SNAKES

a Golden Guide® from St. Martin's Press

Written by Sarah Whittley
Consultant Jock Boyd
Illustrated by
Peter D. Scott/Wildlife Art Ltd.

St. Martin's Press   New York

FOREWORD

The aim of this book is to introduce the reader into the fantastic world of snakes.

Just as the previous Golden Guides from St. Martin's Press have paved the way for good quality, reliable nature guides, *Snakes* continues in this tradition.

Special thanks must go to the artist Peter David Scott; he has worked tirelessly, producing an outstanding collection of exceptional work. Thanks must also go to his wife, Pauline, for her support.

Many people have helped create this book. Thanks to Jock Boyd, David Showler and Van Wallach, Harvard University, for their herpetological expertise, Sylvia Sullivan for editorial, and Reg 'on the' Page and Chris Donaldson for their design skills.

ISBN 0-312-30608-3

First edition: September 2002

CONTENTS

INTRODUCTION

Snakes are fascinating and beautiful members of the Animal Kingdom. These silent and secretive creatures do not deserve the bad press they so commonly receive – out of around 2,700 species only roughly 300 are dangerously venomous, and even then most would need serious provocation to attack.

Snakes can sometimes be confused with lizards. Although they are closely related, there are several differences: no snakes have legs, whereas the majority of lizards do; lizards have eyelids, unlike snakes which have a transparent scale called a brille over their eyes, which is shed with every molt. Most lizards have a visible ear opening – snakes don't. Snakes' jaws also differ in that they are made up of many small delicate bones that move to accommodate the swallowing of prey larger than their gape. Lizards have two lungs whereas most snakes have lost the need for two and use only one.

To move, they have to rely on exceptionally strong muscles and a flexible spine. Snakes usually have a single row of ventral scales called scutes; which aid the snake when moving.

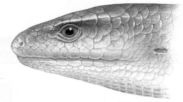

Head of glass lizard (above) and head of snake (right). Snakes have no visible ear opening and instead of eyelids, a transparent scale, called a brille, covers the eyes.

Snakes employ several ways of moving; desert species tend to "sidewind", the loose sand prevents them from getting a good grip, so they throw out loops sideways while pressing their head and tail downwards.

The "caterpillar" crawl allows the snake to move in a straight line by anchoring its belly scutes on any irregularities on the ground, then using its muscles to push up the rest of its body.

With the "serpentine" motion, the scales on the lower flanks push off from bumps on the surface from left to right. Muscles contract and relax on either side of the body, creating the familiar winding motion seen in most species.

"Caterpillar crawl"

"Serpentine" motion

THE ORIGINS AND EVOLUTION OF SNAKES

Snakes first appeared around 140 million years ago during the early Cretaceous period. In reptile terms, this is not very old. Lizards first appeared 250 million years ago and ruled the world for 235 million years. Mammals (which includes us) have been around for only some 65 million years. It is believed that snakes evolved from lizards. For some reason snakes chose a subterranean existence, therefore their bodies had to adapt to life underground. This meant the loss of all unnecessary appendages, like limbs and ear openings. As far as we know, *Lapperentophis defrennei* is the earliest known snake; its fossil remains were found in what is now North Africa. Two of the oldest known snake families are the Boidae (boas) and Pythonidae (pythons). These primitive snakes still have the remnants of their lizard ancestors. They have two tiny bones that were once hind limbs protruding on either side of the body. The bones are covered by a claw and are called spurs.

Pythons and boas have a tiny clawlike spur on either side of the body — the remnants of what were once hind limbs.

However, fossils dating from the late Cretaceous period show that snakes must have traveled far and wide as they are now found on almost every continent. In order to understand the distribution of snakes, it is necessary to understand how the seven continents we know today were formed. Around 250 million years ago, all the continents (or land masses) were grouped together forming one large landmass, called the Pangea. This was surrounded by one giant ocean called Panthalassa. About 200 million years ago, this land mass began to break up, gradually spreading across the globe. By around 65 million years ago, the continents had stopped shifting dramatically and had settled into pretty much the positions that we see today.

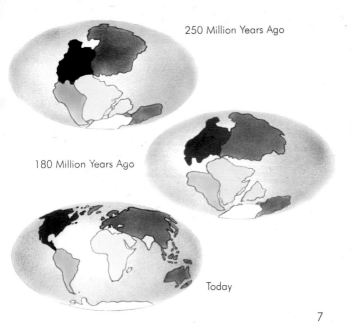

250 Million Years Ago

180 Million Years Ago

Today

INSIDE A SNAKE

THE BODY

During the course of their evolution, snakes have adapted to a completely limbless life. As a consequence their skeletons are fantastically designed. Whereas we have 33 vertebrae in our spine or backbone, snakes have from 180 in smaller species and up to 400 in larger species. The snakes backbone runs the whole length of the body with hundreds of paired ribs attached to it. The backbone is remarkably flexible and strong, the trunk (body) muscles are also very powerful; they would have to be to enable a King Cobra to rear to 6 ft (2 m) or a python to constrict an antelope. The ribs, which run the length of the body, are paired and arch out from each vertebrae. There are many muscles; some connect specialized vertebrae to vertebrae and ribs to ribs. The skin muscles allow the ribs to pull scales forward. A snake's skeleton and skull is made up of many delicate bones, which can be easily damaged.

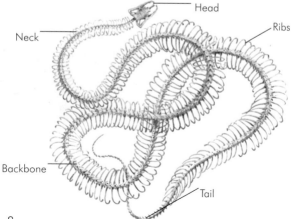

INTERNAL ORGANS

Snakes have internal organs very similar to ours. The major difference is that they have to fit their heart, lungs, kidneys, liver, and stomach into a long, thin body. Snakes, like us, have to breathe air; some of the more primitive snakes, like boas and pythons, have two lungs, although one is always bigger than the other. All other snakes have lost the use of their left lung. In some species of marine snakes, the right-hand lung runs almost the whole length of the snake's body. This useful development ensures that large amounts of air can be stored for prolonged dives. It can act as a buoyancy aid for marine snakes.

The digestive system of a snake starts at its mouth. Food then has some way to travel to reach its stomach, this journey is helped by the strong muscles in the esophagus and throat, which push the food through. Although snakes don't have bladders, they still need to excrete excess fluid. Once the fluid has passed through the kidneys it is expelled as uric acid, which looks like a lump of crystal.

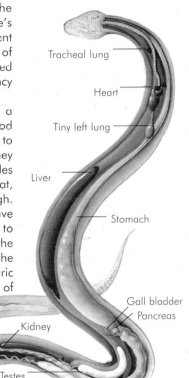

Tracheal lung

Heart

Tiny left lung

Liver

Stomach

Gall bladder
Pancreas

Kidney

Kidney

Testes

TEETH AND FANGS

A hunter without an effective weapon would be pretty useless, so too would a venomous snake without its fangs. This is why all venomous snakes can re-grow or replace their fangs if broken or by natural shedding. If you look closely into their mouths you can sometimes see up to five standby fangs waiting to be used.

Many snakes have in excess of 200 teeth. Usually they are sharp and needle-like and curve towards the back of the mouth. This enables the snake to grab and keep hold of its prey. Some snakes have especially long, curved teeth, like the Wolf Snake, which needs to keep hold of the slippery, smooth-skinned skinks – its favorite food. The Neck-banded Snake has even developed large, flat, knife-like teeth for holding on to skinks.

Snakes can be front-fanged or back-fanged. As a rule, the more evolved the snake (Viperidae and Elapidae) the more likely that they will have front fangs. These snakes are normally venomous and need the front fangs to ensure prey is subdued quickly without causing damage to the snake itself. Most of the colubrids (this family makes up over half of all snake species) are back-fanged and harmless. Only two are dangerously venomous and they are the African Boomslang and Kirtland's Twig Snake.

VENOM

Venom is basically a wonderful mixture of proteins and enzymes. It is important to bear in mind that this sometimes devastatingly lethal mixture is there for snakes' survival and defense, not for killing humans.

Venom can contain neurotoxins, which cause damage to the nervous system, cytotoxins, which destroy cell structure, cardiotoxins, which damage the heart, and hematoxins, which affect blood cells. The enzymes found in venom can cause serious damage to humans, but actually help the snake break down and digest its food. For example, proteinases specialize in destroying proteins and DNase for destroying DNA. Some snakes produce their own specific lethal mixtures. Kraits from the *Bungarus* genus produce Bungarotoxin, Crotoxin is produced by the genus *Crotalus,* which includes rattlesnakes. Snakes generally have one or two predominant toxins in their venom, elapsids tend to be more neurotoxic (attacks nerves) while pit vipers' is more cytoxic (attacks cells).

In the Western world snake bites are not common and fatalities even rarer. In the USA, the most common venomous bites are from pit vipers – usually rattlesnakes and Copperheads.

Venom released through tiny hole in the fang

Venom gland

The venom glands of some vipers are so large, they make the back of the snake's head swollen. This can be seen in the Gaboon Viper. Most snakes have a tiny hole at the rear on the tip of each fang which allows the venom to be injected into prey. However, spitting cobras have these holes on the front of the fangs, allowing the venom to be sprayed forwards.

SENSES

SMELL

There is nothing sinister about the familiar sight of a snake flicking its tongue in and out of its mouth. It is just simply "tasting" the air. Whereas we only use our nose to smell, snakes use their tongues and a sensory device called a Jacobson's organ. As soon

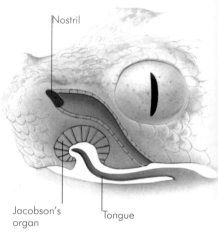

Nostril

Jacobson's organ

Tongue

as the tongue is withdrawn, the tip is placed in the Jacobson's organ which is found in a recess in the top of the mouth; information is then processed by the brain and the snake can decide if an object should be avoided or pursued. The Jacobson's organ is not unique to snakes – all reptiles have one. As well as this organ, snakes have nostrils that connect to the olfactory part of the brain, thus enhancing their sense of smell.

SIGHT

Not all snakes have good eyesight. This is probably due to their burrowing habits, where the use of other senses would have been more useful. The position of the eyes on the head and the shape of the pupils are both important; snakes that hunt by lying in wait in leaf litter need eyes that

Green Tree Python

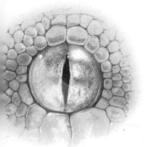

Long-nosed Green Tree Snake

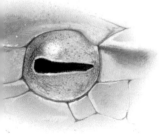

Rough Green Snake

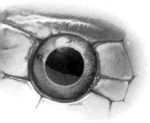

face upwards, while those that hunt by chasing through trees need good forward-facing, binocular vision. The pupils of snakes come in a variety of shapes, from round to horizontal. Some snakes even have camouflaged pupils – the black stripes on Mandarin Ratsnake's pupils, give it a very distinctive look.

HEARING

Unlike other reptiles, snakes don't have external ear openings. This means snakes are unlikely to hear the same airborne sounds that we do. Instead, they have a sophisticated inner ear which enables them to balance and pick up on the smallest of vibrations. However, to do this they must have their lower jaw in contact with the ground or a tree. The vibrations are then transmitted to the inner ear via the small bones in its head. Our approaching footsteps would usually be enough to make sure of a quick exit by most snakes.

HEAT PITS

If you look closely at the head of boas, pythons and pit vipers you can see small holes or pits between the eyes and nostrils. These facial pits are thermal receptors lined with nerves that enable the snake to seek out its warm-blooded prey with remarkable accuracy.

Boas and pythons have many pits which run along the edge of the mouth. Pit vipers have the most highly developed senses of any snake. The warmth emitted by their prey is picked up by the two pits found on either side of their nose. These act in unison, enabling them to gauge the size of their prey and then pinpoint it with stunning accuracy. Heat pits are so sensitive they can also pick up the smallest of temperature change.

Besides facial pits, it is thought that many snakes have thermoreceptors in their scales. This would help the snake recognize and react to touch.

Boas, pythons and pit vipers have heat-sensitive openings on the head which enable them to detect prey.

Heat pits

Above Pythons and boas have heat sensitive pits running down each side of the mouth. *Right* Pit vipers have two characteristic pits towards the front of the head.

14

MOLTING OR SLOUGHING

When the snake's outer layer of skin gets worn out, it grows a new one. A few days before the molt the snake's colors dull, the eyes go cloudy and it gets sluggish and bad-tempered. It usually only takes a few hours for the old skin to be shed. The old skin is normally intact, and can be found discarded on the ground. Freshly molted snakes always look pristine and brightly colored.

File Snake – rough scales

SCALES

Scales grow from the top layer of skin called the epidermis. When the skin is stretched, the skin between the scales can be seen. This expansion is very useful when swallowing large prey. Some snakes, like the Rough-scaled Tree Viper, have keeled or ridged scales, which help them to hang on to their prey or break up their outline when hiding in leaves. File or Wart Snakes have rough, granular bumps covering their body, which help them hang onto their slippery fish prey. Other snakes have very smooth scales, especially the burrowing snakes, which need to slip with ease through soil.

Mexican King Snake – smooth scales

Rattlesnake – keeled scales

15

REPRODUCTION

Most snakes are egg-layers or oviparous but some bear live young. They are called viviparous. Some species don't even need a mate to reproduce!

Viviparous snakes do produce eggs but instead of being laid and left in the nest, like oviparous species, the mother keeps them inside her body until they are ready to experience the outside world. As a general rule, snakes from cooler climates tend to be viviparous; keeping the eggs warm during their gestation enhances their chances of survival. The downside of this is that carrying sometimes as many as 50 or more babies around makes the mother more sluggish and vulnerable to being attacked.

The Brahminy Blind Snake is an example of a parthenogenetic (reproduction without fertilization) species. When the eggs hatch, the offspring are genetically identical to their mother and usually all female. This is the only snake to reproduce this way.

FOOD AND FEEDING

There is no such thing as a vegetarian snake. All snakes, without exception eat other animals. Snakes can be either dietary generalists or specialists. Generalists take a huge variety of prey, e.g. the Black Racer will eat reptiles, birds and birds' eggs, small mammals, amphibians and insects. Some snakes, however, are very specialized eaters; the Thirst Snake from South America eats nothing but snails and Queen Snakes from North America only eat soft-shell crayfish.

Snakes have had thousands of years to perfect their hunting strategies, which make them very efficient predators. There are three basic strategies: the sit and wait approach used by many heavy-bodied vipers; the chase and stab technique used by many fast-moving, active snakes, and the lure, where a snake waves the tip of its tail to entice animals to within striking distance. Once caught, prey is either subdued by venom or by constriction.

Many species of snake use constriction to kill their prey. *Below* African Rock Pythons have been known to tackle prey as fearsome as crocodiles.

SNAKE CLASSIFICATION

Snakes are currently grouped into 18 families. Each family is then divided into genera, which is further divided into species. However, new species are still being discovered and more information collected on recognized species.

Ongoing research may indicate that already known species may in fact be more than one species. In other cases, the opposite may occur, with two or more species being "lumped" as one.

This book looks at each family from the most primitive to the most advanced. After a brief introduction to each family, accounts of representative species follow .

The 18 families are as follows:

LEPTOTYPHLOPIDAE . . thread snakes
ANOMALEPIDAE . . . . . dawn blind snakes
TYPHLOPIDAE . . . . blind snakes
ANOMOCHILIDAE . . . dwarf pipe snakes
ANILIIDAE . . . . South American pipe snake
CYLINDROPHEIDAE . . . Asian pipe snakes
UROPELTIDAE . . . . Shield-tailed snakes
LOXOCEMIDAE . . . . . . New World sunbeam snake
XENOPELTIDAE . . . . . . Asian sunbeam snakes
BOIDAE . . . . boas
PYTHONIDAE . . . . pythons
TROPIDOPHIIDAE . . . . wood snakes
BOLYERIIDAE . . . . Round Island boas
ACROCHORDIDAE . . . wart or file snakes
COLUBRIDAE . . . . colubrids
ATRACTASPIDIDAE . . . . burrowing asps
ELAPIDAE . . . . cobras, kraits, mambas, coral
snakes, sea snakes
VIPERIDAE . . . . vipers

LEPTOTYPHLOPIDAE

This family consists of 86 species in 2 genera: *Leptotyphlops* (85 species), and *Rhinoleptus* with one member, *R. koniagui* of western Africa. Thread snakes look very similar to blind snakes only they are much smaller, a pinky color and almost threadlike, as their name suggests. At a first glance you might mistake these snakes for worms, that's how small they are. In fact, some herpetologists claim that they are not snakes at all but legless lizards, on the basis that they have a well-developed pelvic girdle, vestigial hind limbs, very small scales and no belly scutes. They don't have a left lung, while females lack a left oviduct. Physiologically, they differ from blind snakes in that they have teeth in the lower jaw and non in their rigid upper jaw; normally blind snakes have teeth in their upper jaw

Thread snakes have a wide distribution, occurring in southwest Asia and the New World, preferring semi-arid regions. Basically they can be found wherever there are termites. Being small snakes, they have to be wary of a termite attack. Luckily, thread snakes can produce a pheromone (chemical substance) which fools the termites into believing they are one of them. As with all burrowing snakes, they rarely venture above ground, where they would be extremely vulnerable to predators due to their small size.

WESTERN BLIND SNAKE (see page 20)

Leptotyphlops humilis

This small snake, which is about as thick as a pencil, reaches a maximum length of 16 in (40 cm). It is usually pale brown, pink or purplish, with a silver sheen. The head and tail are blunt, with a spine at the tail tip. Rudimentary eyes appear as spots under the head scales. Teeth are lacking from the upper jaw. The Western Blind Snake occurs from southern California to western Texas and down to Mexico. It is found in all of Baja California and western and north-central Mexico. If disturbed, it will writhe and wiggle its tail to focus attention here instead of on the head. This small serpent shares a feature with the much larger boas and pythons – the remains of a pelvic girdle and femur, complete with a tiny spur! A secretive, nocturnal species, it lays up to 7 eggs in mid-summer. They prefer moist, loose soils suitable for burrowing. This may include the sandy washes or canyon bottoms of brushy mountain areas or desert grasslands.

SCHLEGEL'S BLIND SNAKE

Leptotyphlops nigricans

This tiny pencil-thin snake from South Africa, reaches a maximum length of 16 in (40 cm). It has a blunt, rounded snout and a short blunt tail. The eyes are hidden under scales. Teeth are lacking from the upper jaw, and it has a vestigial pelvic girdle. If disturbed, it will writhe and wiggle its tail to focus attention here instead of on the head. It is preyed upon by a wide variety of animals, including birds, mammals, snakes, fish and even spiders.

It eats mainly ants and termites along with their eggs, pupae, and larvae. Millipedes and centipedes are sometimes eaten. It hunts by locating ant pheromone trails, following them back to the nest and then consuming the residents. The smooth, tightly-overlapping scales provide protection against ant bites. Lays up to 7 eggs in mid-summer.

TEXAS BLIND SNAKE

Leptotyphlops dulcis

Although very similar to the Western Blind Snake, its range extends farther north, from Kansas to Oklahoma southwards to Mexico. It has the misfortune of being used as a cleaner by Eastern Screech Owls. Owls' nests are littered with parasites which cause harm to the owl's young. By picking up a blind snake and placing it in the nest, the owl gets a clean and safe home to raise its owlets and the snake gets a guaranteed, if limited, food source.

ANOMALEPIDAE

Along with the thread and blind snakes, this is our most primitive snake family. It has 4 genera containing around 15 species, all of which are found in Central and South America. Very little is known about these secretive snakes – they live an almost exclusively subterranean life, and it is thought they hunt mainly termites and that they are all egg layers. Unlike other blind snakes, they have one or two teeth in their lower jaw, otherwise they share the features of a typical blind snake. They are not very colorful, usually brown or black, although some do have white heads and tails.

TYPHLOPIDAE

This family comprises 5 genera containing 218 species, including some of our most primitive snakes. They are about 8 in (20 cm) long. They have smooth, shiny scales, and worm-like appearance. All the snakes in this family are burrowing snakes, like the two previous families, and therefore have specially adapted bodies. Although not readily visible, these snakes do have eyes but their eyesight is minimal. Instead they rely on their other senses, smell and touch. Their eyes are hidden under scales and unlike other snakes, lack the spectacle or brille (transparent scales over eyes). Another aspect that makes them different from most snakes is their lack of belly scales or scutes. The scales are also especially smooth, another useful adaptation for a life spent pushing through soil. Another adaptation is the

23

reinforced skull; it is rigid and consists of a single plate. These gentle, harmless snakes survive almost exclusively on a diet of ants and termites. Blind snakes all lay tiny eggs.

BRAHMINY BLIND SNAKE
Ramphotyphlops braminus
Adult size is 2.5–6.5 in (6.5–16.5 cm). It varies in color from brown with a black stripe on the back, to just black-gray. Eyes are dot-like remnants under the scales. Its tail is tipped with a tiny spur. It likes to burrow in damp soil and leaf litter and can usually be found under stones or logs. Although it is native to Southeast Asia, it has been accidently introduced, in plant soil, to USA, Australia and South Africa. IThey are the only "parthenogenetic" snake, which means the females are able to reproduce without the use of the males' sperm. All the eggs hatch into females.

EUROPEAN WORM SNAKE

Typhlops vermicularis

This is a slender snake which looks a little like an earthworm. The head is inconspicuous, not easily distinguishable from the tail, which is short and blunt with a small terminal spine; the mouth is very small. The eyes are underneath the scales, visible as two small black dots. This snake is mainly subterranean. It inhabits damp soils or it may be found under stones. It preys on small invertebrates, especially ants and their larvae. Lays 4–8 eggs. Found in Greece, Albania, southern parts of former Yugoslavia, Bulgaria, a few Greek islands, Cyprus, southwest Asia and northeast Egypt and in mountains up to 1,500–1,600 ft (460–490 m).

Typhlops congestus
This is one of the largest blind snakes, and can grow to just over 3 ft 3 in (1 m). It spends most of its time underground in the forests of Central Africa.

Ramphotyphlops nigrescens
This blind snake is from Australia, and is Australia's only insectivorous snake. It feeds on termites and the eggs, larvae and pupae of ants. It is non-venomous and extremely secretive. It is largely restricted to bushland.

PIPE SNAKES

Once all the pipe snakes were grouped in the Aniliidae family. Now they have been split into 3 families – dwarf, South American, Asian and pipe snakes. Pipe snakes have a nonfunctional pelvis, vestigial hind limbs and a reduced left lung. These snakes differ from other burrowing snakes as they have belly scales. In some ways, they bridge the gap between "primitive" snakes and the more advanced snakes, such as boas. For example, they take larger prey, sometimes prey as large as themselves. However, due to their rigid, fused skull they find it difficult to swallow bulky prey, so they concentrate on long, slender prey items, like snakes and eels. Another interesting feature is their ability to mimic venomous snakes; remember, burrowing snakes don't have venom. This is a real development for such a primitive snake. For example, the Guyanan Pipe Snake lives in the same region as the highly venomous Coral Snake and has very similar coloring. The Malayan Pipe Snake has a great defense strategy: when under threat it flattens its body then waves its tail menacingly in the air, which reveals its crimson underside. This could look like an angry, poisonous snake.

Pipe snakes have a primitive skull structure. Many of the bones are rigid and inflexible, unlike more advanced snakes, such as elapids and vipers.

ANOMOCHILIDAE

Up until recently, these snakes have been grouped with Asian pipe snakes (Cylindropheidae). Now they have been placed in a family on their own. The family has a single genus that contains 2 species; both occur in Borneo, Malaysia and Sumatra. Unlike other pipe snakes, they lay eggs.

ANILIIDAE

SOUTH AMERICAN PIPE SNAKE

Anilius scytale
This snake is the sole member of this genus. It lives in the Amazon basin, burrowing in leaf litter and muddy water. Its known maximum length is 3 ft 3 in (1 m). Its red and black appearance acts as a warning coloration, duping would-be predators that it is as poisonous as the similarly colored and highly venomous Coral Snake. Its small eyes lie beneath a transparent, polygonal scale. It eats eels, caecilians (burrowing, legless amphibians) and frogs. It bears live young, giving birth to 3–13 young.

28

CYLINDROPHEIDAE

All 10 species in the one genus *Cylindrophis* occur in India, Sri Lanka and Southeast Asia. They differ from the Aniliidae family as they have a brille over the eyes. All have boldly marked, black and white undersides and flattened tails. They bear live young. Food includes eels, caecilians and other snakes. What makes these snakes really special is their brilliant self-defense technique. This involves pretending to be a cobra. The snake will curl up, lift its flattened tail tip off the ground and wave it around, in the manner of a cobra with a fully flattened collar, ready to strike.

RED-TAILED PIPE SNAKE

Cylindrophis maculatus
The underside of the tail with black and white markings, contrasts with the reddish-orange markings on its back – enough to confuse any predator!

The Red-tailed Pipe Snake (*C. maculatus*) is endemic to Sri Lanka. It grows up to 28 in (70 cm) long.

29

UROPELTIDAE

There are 8 genera and 47 species in this family. All come from the Indian subcontinent and Sri Lanka. Most prefer mountains except for the *Pseudotyphlops philippinus* of Sri Lanka, which can be found in lowland areas.

Although very similar to pipe snakes, having a reinforced skull, they show no vestiges of the hind limbs and pelvis. The first two vertebrae of the neck have exceptionally flexible joints, allowing the snake to bend its head to an amazingly sharp angle.

These snakes get their name from the bizarre shape of their tails. The shield, which looks rather like a fingernail, is unique among burrowers, which is why it has been placed in a family on its own.

Some of the tails have spines; others are flat, and some look like a broad, flattened disc with rough scales all over. When under attack, they will bury their head under their coiled body and wave their plated tail in the air.

These snakes come in a range of colors, some with brilliant oranges and reds. Length 8–30 in (16–76 cm). They give birth to live young, usually about six, a very small number compared with some snakes. They prey on worms and other soft-bodied invertebrates.

LOXOCEMIDAE

There is only one species in this family, the Neotropical Sunbeam Snake *Loxocemus bicolor*.

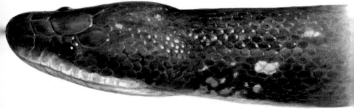

Although superficially very similar to
the Asian Sunbeam Snake (page 32),
the Neotropical Sunbeam Snake has
a shorter and more pointed head.

NEOTROPICAL SUNBEAM SNAKE

Loxocemus bicolor

Otherwise known as the Mexican Burrowing Snake, this
species comes from El Salvador, Mexico and the Pacific
lowlands of Central America. It grows up to 3 ft 3 in (1m)
and can live in a variety of forest habitats. For a long time
scientists didn't know how to classify this mystifying snake;
it shares many similarities with the Asian sunbeam snakes
(Xenopeltidae), yet it looks and behaves more like a python
as it constricts its prey. It has vestiges of a pelvic girdle,
paired lungs, a postfrontal bone and premaxillary teeth.
This gentle, strong-jawed snake is very reluctant to bite.
Although essentially a burrowing snake, it spends some
time above ground hunting lizards, rodents, turtle and
iguana eggs. This snake lays small clutches of eggs.

XENOPELTIDAE

This Old World family has one genus containing 2 species. These snakes have compressed, spade-shaped heads for burrowing and highly glossy, smooth, iridescent scales, which in sunlight are very colorful – hence the name. Superficially they look very similar to their New World counterparts (*Loxocemus*), indeed they share body proportions, iridescent scales, a pair of lungs, premaxillary teeth and a relatively flexible jaw. The differences, however, begin with the lack of the postfrontal bone and no pelvic girdle.

ASIAN SUNBEAM SNAKE

Xenopeltis unicolor
Its flexible lower jaw helps it grasp their prey, which consists of small mammals and skinks. It spends most of its time underground and as a consequence this shy, nocturnal, egg-laying snake is difficult to find.

BOIDAE

This family is divided into two subfamilies (Boinae and Erycinae), containing 7 genera with 36 species. Recently, the Calabar Ground Python, genus *Calabaria* has been re-classified and is now classed as a boa and is placed in the genus *Charina*.

Vestigial reticulated claw, known as a spur

Boas are surely the most familiar and impressive group of snakes. They include some of the largest snakes. Boas and pythons share many similarities; they both constrict their prey and have vestigial hind limbs. However, there are several differences that have meant a re-classification, splitting boas and pythons into two separate families. Boas lack premaxillary teeth, and a supraorbital bone in the head. Pythons have paired scutes under the tail, whereas boas have a single row of scales under the tail. Boas typically have small, smooth scales on the head and body. There is an exception to this in the form of the Rough-scaled Boa, *Eryx conicus*. You can find boas in a mixture of habitats ranging from semi-aquatic to arboreal and underground. With the exception of the Calabor Ground Boa, *Charina reinhardtii*, all give birth to live young. There are no boas in Southeast Asia.

Genus *Boa*
All 4 species are found in Central and South America and
Madagascar.

COMMON BOA
Boa constrictor
This is not the monster of myth and legend; in fact, it is only
the sixth largest snake in the world, around 13 ft (4 m). It
is found in Central and South America and, though not
venomous, can give a very painful bite if molested. It varies
in size and color, with over 10 recognized subspecies. They
all have the classic saddle markings down their backs.
Although these powerful constrictors are most at home on
the ground, they can climb and swim well. This is an
adaptable species that is found in both dry regions and
rainforests. It gives birth to 10–15 live young.

Genus *Corallus*

There are 7 species, all of which are colorful tropical South American boas. All give birth to live young. They are all strong constrictors and are arboreal, seldom coming down to the ground.

EMERALD TREE BOA

Corallus caninus

This tree-dwelling snake has brilliant green coloration that camouflages it among the ferns and other plants of its rainforest habitat. An agile climber, it has a laterally flattened body and a prehensile tail that it uses to grasp branches. It is about 5ft (1.5m) long. The preferred prey is birds and small mammals, but juveniles may target lizards. The females are viviparous, giving birth to 10–18 live young. When they first hatch Emerald Tree Boas are a brick-red color. They stay this way for 2–3 years.

Genus *Epicrates*

RAINBOW BOA

Epicrates cenchria

The Rainbow Boa has iridescent scales which create a similar effect to oil on water. This species has a vast range over most of Central and South America in rainforest, dry woodland and savannah. They are powerful predators that kill their prey by constriction. There are different color forms that can be orange, red or black and various body patterings.

The Rainbow Boa tends to be nocturnal and has heat-sensitive pits. During the day it rests in the trees, but at night it prowls through the trees and the forest edge for its favorite prey of small mammals. It gives birth to 10–30 live young.

Genus *Eunectes*

GREEN ANACONDA
Eunectes murinus

At up to 33 ft (10 m) long, the Green Anaconda is one of the largest living snakes in the world. Although the Reticulated Python may grow longer, the Green Anaconda often grows to an immense weight and huge girth. The early Spanish settlers used to refer to the anaconda as the "matatoro" or "bull killer". The head is quite large and the small eyes have vertical pupils. With nostrils opening on the top of its head and its green and black coloration, the Green Anaconda is perfectly suited to its aquatic habitat.

It prowls its watery world at twilight and at night in pursuit of fish, mammals and birds. Larger specimens will eat capybara, tapir, cayman, crocodiles and even humans, suffocating them in their powerful coils, before eating them head first.

Genus *Charina*

There are three species in this genus: the Rosy Boa and the Rubber Boa from North America and the Calabar Ground Boa (below), the latter has recently been placed in this genus.

CALABAR GROUND BOA

Charina reinhardti

This is a West African species. It is found in Cameroon, Sierra Leone, Liberia, Ivory Coast, Ghana, and through Nigeria. It inhabits temperate rainforest habitats, burrowing in leaf litter and loose soil. Is this a python? Or maybe a boa? Previously it was referred to as a python because it is an egg layer. But now it is referred to as a boa. It prefers moister habitats than the African sand boas (genus *Eryx*). A small species seldom reaching 4 ft (1.2 m) in length, it has a very small head and round eyes with a nose built for burrowing. It tends to curl up into a tight ball, with its head tucked beneath its coils as its tail distracts any intruder by acting like a head. The mouth is very small, which means it struggles to eat anything larger than a mouse.

PYTHONIDAE

There are 8 genera containing 26 species. The boa family may contain the heaviest snake, but the pythons possibly have the longest – the massive Reticulated Python.

The beautiful blend of rich reds, oranges, yellows and browns make pythons exceptionally handsome. These chunky snakes typically have long, lance-shaped heads and some have head pits along the edges of their jaws. As with boas, their eyes have a vertical pupil; this cat-like feature gives them a very distinctive look. They also have two extra bones, called supra-orbitals, in the roof of their skulls. These bones are missing in other, more highly developed snakes.

Pythons have adapted to a number of habitats. However none share the burrowing habits of some boas. Another important feature that separates these two snake families is that pythons lay eggs, and many species brood them as well, which is quite unusual among reptiles. They coil around the eggs, protecting them until they hatch.

Genus *Antaresia*

All 4 Australian pythons are found in this genus.

CARPET PYTHON (see page 40)

Morelia spilota

The Carpet Python is the most widespread of all Australian pythons, and exhibits a variety of patterns. It generally grows to about 6 ft 6 in (2 m). Typically, they are yellow with brown cross-barring but there are at least 6 other sub-species that have different patterns. The northeastern Queensland form is black and yellow with large spots while the form known as the Diamond Python from Sydney has a black edge around every yellow scale, producing a bright, intricate pattern.

Carpet Python

Children's Python

CHILDREN'S PYTHON

Antaresia childreni

This relatively small python, never much more than 3 ft (1 m), is a very strong constrictor. It's not the smallest python; that is the Pygmy Python, *L. perthensis*, which is just under 2 ft (50 cm). The Children's Python (named after J.G. Children) has very prominent, almost bulging eyes. The vertical pupil suggests that it is a nocturnal hunter. It feeds on a variety of animals, including bats, frogs and small mammals. The female incubates her eggs by coiling around them and by slightly raising her body temperature.

Genus *Python*

All of the 7 species in this genus are heavy-bodied constrictors. Some have been known to eat humans. They occur in Africa, Southeast Asia and Australia.

BURMESE PYTHON
Python molurus

This large python, with its distinctive pattern of large blotches outlined in cream or gold, with an arrow shape on top of the head, is easily recognizable. Having one of these around the house, as is often the case in their range, can be a mixed blessing. They keep down vermin but will take chickens, dogs, apparently leopards and there are records of human fatalities. The record length is 23 ft (7 m) but around 13 ft (4 m) is the more usual maximum.

The albino strain of the Burmese Python, *P. molurus bivillatus,* is sometimes called the "Golden Python". It is a favorite among captive breeders and apart from its look, has exactly the same habits.

RETICULATED PYTHON
Python reticulatus

The largest Reticulated Python ever measured was 32 ft 9.5 in (10 m), the record for the longest snake in the world. The Reticulated Python has a complex, geometric pattern, with a series of irregular diamond shapes along its back and a series of smaller markings with light centers along its flanks. This gives the snake a netlike pattern, which is how it gets its common and Latin name. This provides excellent camouflage in the steamy, tropical rainforests of Southeast Asia.

Reticulated Pythons are expert ambush predators, often waiting in trees for unsuspecting prey such as large mammals like monkeys and pigs. They are opportunistic hunters and will come down from the relative safety of the trees to catch rats, domestic fowl and, on rare occasions,

human prey. An interesting fact about this snake is its ability to consume large deer, even those with antlers. If the antlers are small enough they are simply swallowed as they are; however if they are too large, the snake can snap them back to lie along the victim's body, allowing them to be engulfed when the animal is consumed.

Females brood their eggs. They lay 30–100 eggs and as the eggs are developing, females will coil around them and "shiver", producing muscle contractions, which increases the overall temperature of the eggs. Females will also defend their eggs against predators. However, once the eggs hatch, the 2 ft (60 cm) long babies are on their own.

Genus *Morelia*

A disputed genus from Australia and nearby islands. There are currently 7 species in this genus.

GREEN TREE PYTHON

Morelia viridis

Juveniles have yellow or red bodies with black-edged white markings. As they reach adulthood these markings change color dramatically. Adults become bright green with white, yellow or light blue flecks along the body, with a yellow underside. This arboreal species likes to wrap around a branch high in the tree canopy, securing itself with the aid of its prehensile tail. Juveniles can use the tail as a lure to attract lizards. Adults prefer a diet of small mammals. Found in New Guinea and northern Australia. Lays 6–30 eggs.

TROPIDOPHIIDAE

This family comprises 4 genera containing 21 species. The bulk of this bizarre family is found in the Caribbean region, and Central and South America. These snakes possess some really weird defense displays. If attacked, wood snakes can autohemorrhage, which means they can bleed profusely through various blood vessels located in their eyes and mouths. They also curl up into a ball, with their head hidden, and then secrete a strong-smelling musk from their anus. Mainly nocturnal, some species change color, to become paler at night.

Genus
Tropidophis
16 species,
all from
South
America
and the
West Indies.

HAITIAN WOOD SNAKE

Tropidophis haetianus
Found on the
Caribbean island
of Haiti, this snake is
equally at home on the
ground or in the branches of trees hunting for lizards.
It also eats mammals and nesting birds.

CUBAN WOOD SNAKE

Tropidophis melanurus

Not all are as colorful as this bright orange specimen. There are two color forms; this color and the more common dark brown with even darker marking along the back. This is one of the largest wood snakes; it can measure up to 3 ft 4 in (1 m), although the majority are much smaller. Cuba has many species of wood snake; there are 11 similar-looking species ranging from gray to brown, but none of the others have the orange color form. As with other wood snakes, they constrict their prey, which consists of birds, frogs, lizards and rodents. These shy, live-bearing snakes use the tip of their tail to lure their prey to within grabbing distance.

Genus *Trachyboa*

Otherwise known as Eyelash Boas, there are 2 species from Central and South America.

EYELASH DWARF GROUND BOA

Trachyboa boulengeri

These are beautifully distinctive snakes, with short, thick-set bodies and with a cluster of scales over their eyes, which look like eyelashes. They also have a hornlike scale on their snout. Most of their time is spent on the forest floor in search of frogs.

Genus *Ungaliophis*
BANANA BOA

Ungaliophis continentalis

The Banana Boas are so called as they have been known to accidentally get transported in bunches of bananas. They spend a lot of time in trees, probably keeping safe in amongst the warmth of the bananas. They come from Central America and eat lizards, frogs and small mammals. This shy snake has striking black ovals with a white outline running down its back.

BOLYERIIDAE

There are 2 genera with 2 species in this family. Of the two species, only the Keel-scaled Boa is thought to survive, sadly the other is thought to be extinct. Both come from Round Island in the Indian Ocean. For a long time these snakes were classed as a subfamily of boas. However, research has proved that they show some fundamental differences. Unlike boas, they have a much-reduced left lung, they also lack the pelvic girdle and have no vestiges of hind limbs.

Another feature that makes these snakes a mystery to herpetologists is their origin. No one really knows where they come from. What we do know is that they are only found on a small island north of Mauritius, in the Indian Ocean. The introduction of goats and rabbits has meant widespread habitat loss, which has had a devastating effect on the snakes.

ROUND ISLAND KEEL-SCALED BOA

Casarea dussumieri
Juveniles are olive brown, but adults are gray with paler marks on the sides. Adults can reach 5 ft (1.5m) in captivity but probably only 3 ft 3 in (1m) in the wild. These egg-laying, nocturnal hunters feed exclusively on lizards.

ACROCHORDIDAE

This family contains a single genus – *Acrochordus* – with just 3 species. They can be found in either fresh or coastal waters. The best way to visualize these snakes is to put your hand into an old woollen sock, and wave it around in a slow and methodical way. Out of the water they are exceptionally sluggish, due to the fact that they have a very low metabolic rate – about half that of other snakes. These aquatic "socks" are called "wart snakes" due to the small granular scales that cover the body. These nocturnal snakes are effectively useless out of the water, preferring to rest hidden amongst watery margins or under fallen trees. When in the water they are excellent hunters; they are fast swimmers and are surprisingly acrobatic. Their coarse, rasping scales help them catch and hold prey. They will grab either a frog or a fish in their mouth or they can use their bodies to seize the prey. Once caught, prey is killed by constriction. Other food taken includes crustaceans and eels. All three species give birth to live young.

JAVAN FILE OR ELEPHANT'S TRUNK SNAKE

Acrochordus javanicus

This aquatic giant can reach over 6 ft long (2 m). It can have a girth of around 1 ft (30 cm). It can be found in fresh water throughout Southeast Asia, Papua New Guinea and Australia.

COLUBRIDAE

This is the largest and most diverse of all snake families. There are 305 genera containing about 1,858 species. They share a selection of fundamental features: all lack a functional left lung, the coronoid bone (the small bone in the jaw present in other more primitive snakes) and any remnants of a pelvis.

The majority have large, symmetrical, platelike scales on their heads, similar to cobras. Many herpetologists view colubrids as the link between the more primitive snakes, like boas and pythons, and the more advanced families like cobras and vipers. Whatever they are, they are certainly worthy of maximum respect due to their successful adaptation to a wide variety of habitats, occupying nearly every corner of the globe, with the exception of very cold areas. They also represent over half of the world's population of snake species. They have a variety of hunting techniques from constriction to venom-delivery. Their habitats range from desert to freshwater lakes. Nearly all lay eggs, but some bear live young, especially those from colder climates.

Although the majority are harmless, a small number have venom-delivering back fangs – but most represent no danger to humans. There are two exceptions: the first is the Boomslang (*Dispholidus typus*) from Africa – it carries a very potent venom which can be lethal to humans; the second is the Kirtland's Twig Snake (*Thelotornis kirtlandii*) also found in Africa.

Genus *Ahaetulla* (Asian Vine Snakes or Long-nosed Tree Snakes)

There are 8 species in this genus. All have forward facing eyes with horizontal pupils. They are completely arboreal and come from Southeast Asia, India and China.

ASIAN VINE SNAKE

Ahaetulla prasina

This back-fanged snake is about 4 ft 6 in (1.4 m) long and gives birth to 3–23 live young.

LONG-NOSED TREE SNAKE

Ahaetulla nasuta

This beautifully elegant snake is extremely thin and up to 6 ft 6 in (2 m) long. Its head is characteristically long with a very pointed snout. The Long-nosed Tree Snake may be gray or green. Its most striking feature is that, coupled with grooves that run along the snout, it has horizontal pupils and can focus its eyes in a forward direction, giving excellent binocular vision. This binocular vision allows it to see better than other snakes, a useful adaptation when hunting fast-moving, camouflaged, arboreal lizards high in the trees. These snakes can either lie in wait for their prey, motionless on a branch for hours on end, with the front part of their body suspended in mid-air, or pursue their prey through the branches of the trees with lightning speed and agility.

Genus *Arizona*

GLOSSY SNAKE

Arizona elegans

The Arizona Glossy Snake is one of the most common snakes of the desert, but most people rarely see them because they are nocturnal. Other habitats include dry grassland and scrub forest. They are found from the western USA to the northern Mexico region. The glossy snake is often referred to as the "faded snake" due to the faded appearance of its coloration, which can be light brown to light gray with dull blotches of tan or gray. These snakes are smooth with glossy scales. They have a prominent eye stripe with slightly vertical pupils. Juveniles are similar to adults, but their blotches are darker. They can grow to over 5 ft (1.5 m) and kill their prey by constriction.

Genus *Bogertophis* (Ratsnakes)

The 2 ratsnakes in this genus were formerly placed in the genus *Elaphe*. They are now however, classed on their own. They are the Trans-Pecos Ratsnake, *Bogertophis subocularis* and *Bogertophis rosaliae*. Both species are found in southern USA and northern Mexico. They can lay up to 20 eggs in one clutch. These snakes feed mainly on small mammals, especially rodents, and birds. They kill their prey by constriction and are active mainly at night.

TRANS-PECOS RATSNAKE
Bogertophis subocularis

This snake comes in two colors. The snake shown is its typical form, which is a buff-brown base color with bold dark brown joined up "H" markings running down its back, usually becoming more boldly marked towards its tail. The other more unusual form is much paler, with the markings and background color washed out. This elegant, slender snake can grow up to 6 ft 6 in (2 m). It spends much of its time by night in and out of rodent holes looking for food. By day it avoids the searing heat of the Chihuahuan Desert by hiding in animal burrows and is well adapted to its surrounding habitat. It lives in rocky semi-desert and dry mountainsides. Its flattened flanks form a pair of ridges where they join the underside of its body, thus making it easier to "climb" over rocks. The belly scales are white and very smooth; this helps the snake move over sand.

Genus *Boiga*

This large genus has 30 species. All are egg-layers and most prefer wooded and mangrove habitats. They have a wide distribution from Africa and Southeast Asia to northern Australia.

GREEN-EYED CAT SNAKE

Boiga cyanea

The tropical rainforests of Southeast Asia have green cats prowling through the trees – not the furry kind, but the long thin slithery kind. Green-eyed Cat Snakes have eyes with vertical pupils, like those of a cat, hence the name. They have bright green scales, with a blue throat and black in between the scales. This 5–6 ft (1.6–1.9 m) snake hunts at night through the branches high in the trees looking for small mammals, lizards and birds to kill with its venom. If the prey is small enough the snake can constrict its prey with a deadly embrace, before swallowing it whole.

When threatened, it will scare its troublesome intruder away with a fearsome, gaping mouth, exposing the black interior. This can give the snake enough time to escape through the branches of its forest home to safety. It lays 4–13 eggs and when the young hatch they have red bodies with a green head.

MANGROVE SNAKE
Boiga dendrophila

This stunning snake from Southeast Asia grows up to 7ft (2.5m) and eats mainly birds, reptiles, frogs and mammals.

The Mangrove Snake has very large eyes with vertical pupils and smooth glossy scales that give it a satiny finish. It is one of the largest arboreal snakes in Asia and is found in the rainforest edge and mangrove swamps. It has a very large mouth with rear-positioned fangs. Prey is immobilized by a mild venom, which is injected with the aid of their grooved teeth. Favorite foods are birds and their eggs, and medium-sized mammals such as squirrels, which it hunts with great agility at night in the tree tops. The females lay 10–14 eggs and the incubation period is about 3 months. When under threat, it will open its mouth to show the bold yellow and black markings on the edge.

Genus *Chilomeniscus* (Sand Snakes)

There are 4 species in the USA. All are egg-layers and live in sandy habitats.

BANDED SAND SNAKE

Chilomeniscus cinctus

This beautiful snake lives in the Sonoran Desert in south-western North America, and is also found on small islands in the Gulf of California. This pretty little snake is an excellent "sand swimmer", spending most of its time just under the desert sand's surface, in a perpetual quest for insect larvae and other underground morsels. Beneath the sand it is considerably cooler than on top of the sun-scorched sands.

Genus *Chionactus* (Shovel-nosed Snakes)

Both species come from the desert regions of southwest USA. Their specially shaped heads help them to "swim through the sand".

SONORAN SHOVEL-NOSED SNAKE

Chionactis palarostris

This snake is 10–17 in (25–43 cm) long, with dark and light bands and a shovel-shaped snout. The body is whitish or yellow in color with black, yellow (or whitish) and red crossbands. Like other shovel-nosed snakes, this species is harmless to humans. It is a snake of arid lands and occurs in upland desert and the Sonoran Desert. Here the ground surface may be rocky or sandy. Lays a clutch of 2–4 eggs. Eats spiders, centipedes, scorpions, cockroaches, crickets and other insects.

The shovel-shaped snout helps this snake push through sand.

Genus *Chrysopelea* (Flying or Tree Snakes)

All 5 species in this genus are completely arboreal. They live in the tops of trees, gliding from one to another with their specially adapted bodies.

FLYING TREE SNAKE

Chrysopelea ornata

This is the largest of the flying snakes. It does not actually fly or glide, but instead performs a sort of parachute jump. It is thin, mildly venomous and back-fanged and can be over 3 ft 3 in (1 m) long. It is found in lowland rainforests of Asia from India to southern China and the Philippines, down the Malay Peninsula to Indonesia. Flying snakes fly by sucking in their guts to form a U-shaped half-cylinder along the entire length of their bodies. The outer edges of their belly scales are rigid while the central portion of their belly scales fold upwards. This concave surface acts like a parachute, and increases air resistance to prolong the "flight".

Genus *Coluber* (Whip Snakes and Racers)

The genus *Coluber* is one of the few snake genera to be found in both the New and Old Worlds. In Europe they are known as whipsnakes, while the single species found in North America is known as a racer. They are all long, slender and agile snakes that can move rapidly through light vegetation or scrub.

HORSESHOE SNAKE

Coluber hippocrepis

Horseshoe Whip Snakes are found in southeast Iberia, Sardinia, Malta, Sicily, and northwest Africa. This snake's common name derives from the markings on the sides of its neck that look like horse-shoes. The snake is very variable in color. It is usually found in dry stony areas sparsely dotted with scrub. Basking takes place in the morning and late afternoon, otherwise the snake usually shelters within rodent burrows, under stones or in loose stone embankments. Although terrestrial, it can climb well and if threatened it will usually flee, but will occasionally hiss loudly in an attempt at intimidation.

Genus *Coronella* (Smooth Snakes)

There are 2 species in this genus: *C. austriaca* and the Southern Smooth Snake (*C. Girondica*) from North Africa.

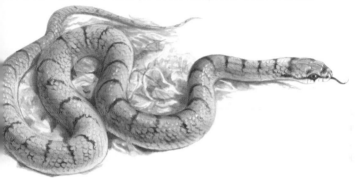

SMOOTH SNAKE

Coronella austriaca

A small snake, 20–24 in (50–60 cm) and highly variable in color and markings. The base color can be either brown, gray, or reddish brown with dark markings running from head to tail. The top of the head shows a heart-shaped mark; this can lead to identification confusion with the Adder. This gentle snake is Britain's rarest reptile; it only occurs in a few southern counties, where it is heavily protected. Smooth snakes are found in dry places, such as heath and open woodland. They hunt by day above and below the ground, disappearing into holes looking for food. Rodents make up around a third of their diet; they much prefer lizards, including Slow Worms. Once caught, the prey is constricted. Although their eyesight is poor, smooth snakes are quick to pick up on movement.

Genus *Dispholidus*
The Boomslang is the only species in this genus.

BOOMSLANG
Dispholidus typus

What makes this snake different from most colubrids is its highly venomous rear-fanged bite. This slim, elegant snake grows to a maximum of about 4 ft 11 in (1.5 m). The Boomslang eats other lizards and occasionally birds. Identification can sometimes be confusing as the colors and markings are variable. Juveniles are a grayish brown, while females are olive-brown. Boomslang is simply Afrikaans for "tree snake".

Genus *Dayspeltis* (Egg-eating Snakes)

All 6 species come from Africa and Arabia. These snakes have numerous specially adapted features to eat their favorite food – eggs. They can swallow an egg three times the diameter of their own heads. The skin around their neck and lower jaw is very elastic, so it can stretch to an amazing degree to allow the egg to pass through. Teeth are not necessary tools for egg-eaters, which is why their mouths are almost toothless. Instead, tiny teeth are embedded in hard, thick gums. Once an egg is found, the snake will flick its tongue over the egg to decide whether or not it is rotten (it prefers fresh eggs), then the snake works its mouth over the egg until it is swallowed; this can sometimes take up to 20 minutes. Once in the throat, the egg is moved back and forth, then special "gular" teeth, which are in fact neck vertebrae, crush the egg shell. The liquid from inside the egg is then pushed towards the stomach, while the crushed shell is regurgitated and ejected from the mouth.

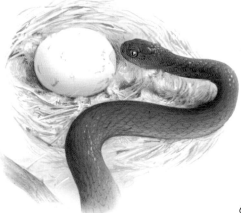

As these snakes have no venom and hardly any teeth, they are vulnerable to attack by mongoose and other snake-eating animals. Their best defense is to mimic poisonous snakes; they imitate Adders by puffing up, hissing and making wild strikes with open mouths.

These nocturnal egg-layers are great climbers.

SOUTHERN BROWN EGG-EATER
Dasypeltis inornata
This snake is very similar in looks and behavior to the Common Egg-eater, *D. Scabra*. It is a little longer, usually just over 3 ft 3 in (1 m). The females lay between 8–17 eggs. These are laid in several different locations; so they must know the problems of egg predation!

Genus *Dipsas* (Thirst Snakes or Snail-eaters)

There are 33 species of Thirst Snakes. They come from Central and South America and all have a specialized diet of snails and slugs. They have a very unusual modification to their jaw to help them extract snails from their shells. They have a very short upper jaw with only five teeth, with these they hold the shell in place while the lower jaw can be thrust forwards into the snail's shell, making it easier to remove their slimy prey from its hard shell. The snakes are nocturnal and have wide, blunt heads with large eyes that have vertical pupils. They lay 2–6 eggs in the leaf litter in the fork of a tree or in a tree hollow.

CATESBY'S SNAIL-EATING SNAKE

Dipsas catesbyi

This small, thin, boldly marked snake lives in the Amazon basin and grows up to 2 ft 3 in (70 cm). Its slender shape enables it to move freely through vegetation in search of its favorite prey, snails.

Genus *Elaphe*
(Ratsnakes and Racers)

These powerful non-venomous constrictors feed on a variety of prey, but mostly rodents. Commonly found on the ground looking for prey in burrows. When under threat, they will coil up and strike repeatedly at the tormentor, while rapidly vibrating the tail.

EUROPEAN LEOPARD SNAKE

Elaphe situla

One of the most striking and beautiful snakes in Europe. It is very similar to the well-known North American Corn Snake, *Elaphe guttata*. Despite its wide range, it is not abundant, and it may be that its conspicuous markings have made it an easy target for snake collectors. It prefers dry, stony areas and deep shady valleys with fast-flowing streams. It is very much a lowland snake, not being found above 1,950 ft (600 m). In June females lay 2–7 eggs in holes in the ground: the hatchlings measure about 12–13 in (30–33 cm).

CORN SNAKE

Elaphe guttata

These attractive snakes are fast-moving, slim, nocturnal hunters with an ability to climb trees, enter burrows and patrol chicken barns in search of food. They will climb trees to look for birds' nests, eggs and juveniles. They are just as at home on or under the ground, where they search for mice, rats and lizards. They usually reach 3 ft 3 in (1 m) although there have been several records of much larger individuals. They can be found in southern and southeastern parts of the USA from south New Jersey to Florida and Louisiana. As a popular "pet" snake, they have been selectively bred and come in a variety of colors. In the wild their colors are less variable.

Genus *Erythrolamprus* (False Coral Snakes)

There are 6 species in the genus and they are found in parts of Central and South America. These back-fanged, mildly venomous snakes have a coral pattern of bright colors along their body that is very similar to the very venomous species of South American coral snake such as the Mayan Coral Snake in the genus *Micrurus*. This is said to be an obvious example of warning color mimicry (called Batesian mimicry). The harmless False Coral Snake looks like the venomous Coral Snake and having the same warning colors helps to warn off any predators.

FALSE CORAL SNAKE

Erythrolamprus aesculapii

There are many similar looking snakes found in the Americas. This one measures 2 ft 3 in (70 cm) and is found in the Amazon Basin, north Trinidad to Ecuador. It lives a very secretive life among rainforest litter on the forest floor.

Genus *Gonyosoma*

Sometimes referred to as racers, this genus comes from southeast Asia. There are 4 species and all are green. Although non-venomous, they are fierce snakes and readily attack if disturbed.

RED-TAILED RACER

Gonyosoma oxycephala

The bright green color of this slender snake helps it to camouflage itself amongst foliage in trees. Each bright green, smooth scale is edged with black. There is also a black eye-stripe running from nose to neck, which separates the dark green area above from the lighter green below. The tail color can vary from dark brown, red or gray-brown. If these snakes feel threatened, they will lift up their heads, and flatten their necks to make them look twice as big. If this fails, a painful bite follows. Another feature of this and other *Gonyosoma* species is their blue tongue.

Genus *Heterodon* (Hog-nosed Snakes)

The genus *Heterodon* is endemic to North America. These heavily built snakes have an unusual defense. When they are threatened, they flatten their neck and head (like cobras), blow up their body, and hiss while striking at the attacker repeatedly. If this fails the snake plays dead, rolling onto its back with its tongue hanging out and emitting a foul, rotting-flesh smell from its cloaca, thus adding to the ruse.

EASTERN HOG-NOSE

Heterodon platyrhinos

Sometimes called the American Puff Adder because of the way it defends itself against attackers. It has a wide, broad head and a fat body with a slightly upturned and shovel-shaped snout, which it uses to dig out its favorite prey — toads. Once it has dug out its prey, the snake deflates the ever-expanding toad with its large back teeth. This bite has a mild venom that subdues the prey. It is then eaten, usually head-first. When threatened, it will play dead by lying on its back with its mouth wide open.

Genus *Lampropeltis* (King Snakes)

There are 8 species in this genus from the Americas. Most are brightly colored and active both day and night.

MEXICAN KINGSNAKE

Lampropeltis mexicana

Although very similar in shape and size to the Gray-banded King Snake (below right) the Mexican King Snake (below left) can be incredibly variable in color and markings. These smooth-scaled snakes are found in northeast Mexico. They lay eggs and eat small mammals and birds. The red markings "saddle" the body.

GRAY-BANDED KINGSNAKE

Lampropeltis alterna

The Gray-banded King (above right) is usually just a little larger, 2 ft 7 in (80 cm), than *L. mexicana*, 2 ft 3 in (70 cm). It is found in desert scrub and rocky canyons in Texas and northern Mexico. This species was first recognized in 1950 and since then has become a favorite for collectors. These shy snakes do not like being handled; they will secrete a foul-smelling odor and thrash about wildly until released.

COMMON KINGSNAKE

Lampropeltis getulus

This common snake is found throughout the southern half of North America. There is much color and pattern variation throughout its range, although basically its chocolate-brown base color is interrupted with biscuit-colored bands. These large, strong snakes can be up to 6 ft 6 in (2 m) long. They won't think twice about eating other snakes, even highly venomous ones such as Copperheads and rattlesnakes; they even have immunity to their venom. Common Kings can be found in a variety of habitats from swamp to desert. These highly adaptable snakes are egg-layers.

Genus *Lamprophis* (House Snakes)

This genus comprises 14 species of elegant and graceful smooth-scaled nocturnal hunters. They come from Africa and the Seychelles and all lay eggs.

AURORA HOUSE SNAKE

Lamprophis aurora

The smooth scales and long thin head give this snake a characteristic appearance. Not a big snake, usually around 1 ft 7 in to 1 ft 11 in (50–60 cm). The adult coloring varies from olive-brown to olive-green, but all have a thin orange dorsal line and a yellowish underside. Juveniles tend to be a brighter green with a more pronounced orange dorsal line. These snakes make the ideal pest control. They are not venomous (they kill their prey by constriction) and they love to eat rodents – making these snakes the perfect house guest. This South African snake lays clutches of 8–14 eggs.

Genus *Malpolon*

There are 2 species in this genus, *M. monspessulanus* and *M. moilensis*. They are egg-layers and come from Europe, North Africa and the Middle East.

MONTPELLIER SNAKE

Malpolon monspessulanus

This large, stiff-bodied snake has an angry-looking face due to the ridge that runs from the back of the head and over large eyes with big pupils. Not only does it look angry, it can be rather an aggressive snake. It moves incredibly quickly and is easily provoked into biting. A large snake, sometimes reaching 6 ft 7 in (2 m), it can take large prey. It has excellent eyesight which it uses to hunt down small mammals such as rabbits and rats. Prey is immobilized by venom; the snake pins down larger prey with its body. As it is rear-fanged it is unlikely to effectively bite humans. A localized swelling and a small amount of discomfort will occur after prolonged bites.

Genus *Masticophis* (Coachwhips)

The coachwhip snakes have very slender bodies with extremely thin whiplike tails. There are 10 species in this genus. They are very variable in color, from black to buff and plain to striped. Highly active snakes, they rely on vision to hunt their small mammal, lizard and bird prey. Found throughout America in various types of habitats, from prairies and deserts to woodland and farmland. Their common name comes from the myth that they chase their prey, tie it to a tree with their coils and whip it until it dies.

CALIFORNIA WHIPSNAKE

Masticophis lateralis
Otherwise known as the Striped Racer, this slender snake hunts by day and is constantly on the move looking for insects and mammals. It grows up to 5 ft (1.6m).

Genus *Natrix* (Eurasian Water Snakes)

The scientific name of this genus is *Natrix*, which means 'water snake', and even though you are more likely to find one near water, they can be found in a variety of terrestrial habitats. They are great swimmers, the head and neck always kept above the water, but if threatened they will dive.

Grass Snakes can vary greatly in color. The yellow collar is characteristic, but sometimes, especially in mature females, it isn't obvious.

GRASS SNAKE

Natrix natrix

This reasonably large water snake comes in a variety of colors. Grass Snakes are usually a shade of olive-green, but brown and gray snakes are not uncommon and some populations in northern Europe may have black individuals. Their bodies bear fine black vertical bars and/or spots running along their sides. Most have a characteristic yellow, sometimes orange, or white collar around the neck. Mature females can be up to 5 ft (150 cm) long, but usually to 4 ft (120 cm).

Diet comprises fish, frogs and small mammals. Grass Snakes start to emerge from hibernation in March and April and mating soon occurs. The female lays 10–40 eggs in June/July. Favorite places include piles of vegetation, manure and compost heaps where the warmth from decomposition helps incubation. Often several females can share the same egg-laying site. The young snakes hatch in August/September. Although they can bite if handled, they are harmless to humans.

Genus *Oxybelis* (Vine Snakes from the Americas)

There are 5 arboreal species found in North, Central and South America. All lay eggs.

MEXICAN VINE SNAKE

Oxybelis aeneus

This incredibly slim snake could easily be mistaken for a twig, which is a great adaptation in a species that spends all its time in trees and shrubs. This snake, about 5 ft (1.5 m) long, can move quickly and silently in search of lizards, especially Anole Lizards. Once caught, lizards are bitten by the snake's back-fangs and are quickly subdued by the venom. Found throughout Arizona south to Mexico and Brazil. In an attempt to startle predators, it will open its mouth wide, revealing a bright purple lining. It is not thought to be dangerous to humans.

Genus *Pareas* (Asian Slug-eaters)

All 5 species are slug and snail eaters. Their jaws are specially modified to deal with their shelled prey. They don't have the fold of skin beneath their chins unlike many other snakes, probably because they don't need to open their mouths very wide to swallow their prey.

ASIAN OR WHITE-SPOTTED SLUG SNAKE

Pareas margaritophopus

This nocturnal snake lives in the moist rainforests of Southeast Asia. They have short, wide heads and blunt snouts and jaws perfectly adapted to remove snails from their shells. They are arboreal and their slender shape enables them to move over very fine vegetation and span wide gaps between twigs in search of their prey. They lay 2–8 eggs in hollow logs or other concealed areas.

Genus *Thelotornis* (Twig Snakes)

There are 2 species of twig snake, Kirtland's Twig Snake, *T. Kirtlandi and* the Bird Snake, *T. capensis, which* occurs in eastern and South Africa. They have extremely thin bodies with lance-shaped heads, large eyes with keyhole-shaped pupils. Both occur in Africa and have a completely arboreal existence within the forests. They rely on their cryptic markings and ambush hunting skills to catch their prey.

KIRTLAND'S TWIG SNAKE

Thelotornis kirtlandi

This snake comes from Central and West Africa. It has very similar habits to its relative the Bird Snake. It grows to 3ft 3 in (1 m) and eats a wide variety of prey, including birds, frogs, lizards and even other snakes. When annoyed it will inflate its neck, which exaggerates its bold markings. This is one of the two highly venomous colubrids. Its venom is hematoxic and although bites are rare, they have caused human fatalities. As these snakes are back-fanged, they must rely on chewing the victim to ensure the venom is injected.

Genus Pituophis (Gopher, Pine and Bull Snakes)

There are 5 species and 15 subspecies. They are usually cream with black patches on their back and a small pointed snout. Most pine-gopher snakes are large and powerful constrictors. When threatened they scare their attackers by shaking their tail and hissing loudly. Because of this, they are sometimes mistaken for rattlesnakes.

LOUISIANA PINE SNAKE

Pituophis ruthveni

These snakes look very similar to their relatives the Kansas bull snakes. Their background color is beige-yellow with dark brown and russet markings. They are becoming very rare in North America, under threat from human encroachment. They have specific habitat requirements – mature longleaf pine forests with loose, sandy soil. They eat gophers, moles, mice and other burrowing rodents. Maximum length nearly 6 ft 6 in (2 m). They have the largest hatchlings of any snake in the USA.

Genus *Sibon* (South American Slug-eaters)

All of the 13 species in this genus prey on slugs and snails. They all lay eggs and live in Central and South America.

CLOUDY SLUG-EATER

Sibon nebulata

Very secretive and nocturnal, these snakes live in deciduous, tropical evergreen and rainforest of central and north South America. A small snake, roughly 31 in (80 cm). Although arboreal, it can be found hiding beneath rotting logs. The best time to find them is on a wet night, when they will be out looking for slugs and snails.

Genus *Thamnophis*
(New World Garter and Ribbon Snakes)

The garter and ribbon snakes are best known for their striking longitudinal stripes that run down their bodies. Some are semi-aquatic and can be seen swiftly gliding across the surface of the water. They are active during the day and they have large eyes with which to find their aquatic prey. They give birth to live young.

EASTERN GARTER SNAKE

Thamnophis sirtalis

Otherwise called the Red-sided Garter Snake, this medium-sized dark brown or black snake has a yellow or gray stripe running along its back, with two other yellow stripes on either side. Some have a red coloring between the side scales – hence the alternative name. The back scales are strongly keeled. These harmless snakes are quite common across most of the USA. They will frequently emerge from hibernation to bask in the sunshine on winter days.

Genus *Tantilla*
(Black-headed and Crowned Snakes)

This large genus has 60 species. These small snakes are all very secretive, and most have a characteristic black head and are found throughout the Americas.

PLAINS BLACK-HEADED SNAKE

Tantilla nigriceps

A small snake, 7–15 in (18–40 cm) with large rear teeth that eats mainly centipedes and scorpions. It may be found in a variety of habitats, ranging from shortgrass prairie to juniper woodlands. They have been known to visit basements but these shy, nocturnal snakes are harmless. Found in Kansas, Texas, Arizona, and Mexico. It only produces a few eggs, 1–3 in each clutch, but, living in places where the climate is mild, it can produce clutches nearly all year round. This means that over the year they can produce as many eggs as other species that lay one large clutch each year.

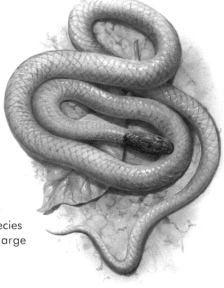

ATRACTASPIDIDAE

There are 8 genera containing 62 species in this family. For a long time these snakes were classified with vipers. They exhibit varied dentition and biting mechanisms. Some have hollow, movable front-mounted fangs, while others have fixed grooved fangs towards the rear of the mouth.

Although the majority are harmless to humans, some species have a potent venom like the Natal Black Snakes whose venom can cause loss of consciousness. Bites from some Atractaspididae can be far more serious since they deliver neurotoxic venom (venom that attacks the nervous system and impairs blood circulation), similar to the venom of vipers and cobras.

As their name suggests nearly all are burrowing species and have therefore suitably adapted bodies. They are generally small to medium-sized, slender, cylindrical snakes with smooth shiny scales. They have a compact skull, some having an obvious snout. Although they have eyes, they tend to be very small. Their tail is short and some species have a protruding spine at its tip.

Burrowing asps are a predominantly African species, with the exception of one species from the Middle East. Nearly all give birth to live young, except the Jackson's Centipede-eater, *Aparallactus jacksonii*.

Genus *Aparallactus* (Centipede-eaters)

As their name might suggest, these specialized feeders have a favorite food. Whereas other burrowing asps typically eat a variety of food, *Aparallactus* has a niche market. These small burrowing snakes grow to a maximum of about 2 ft (60 cm) and spend much of their time in sandy soil, old termite nests and other rotting debris. All of the centipede-eaters are found in Africa, from the south of the Sahara down to South Africa. Their teeth are well designed for preying on centipedes; they have enlarged fangs for grabbing a centipede, which in Africa can be huge, sometimes over 5 in (12 cm) long and almost twice the diameter of the snake! The smaller teeth in the mouth help to keep hold of the writhing giant. Once the snake has subdued the centipede with its venom, it is then able to swallow it whole. Many of these giant centipedes are extremely poisonous, some carrying enough poison to kill a human, however, the centipede-eaters are completely resistant to the poison. Although poisonous, centipede-eaters are rear-fanged small snakes, not harmful to humans.

Genus *Atractaspis*
(Stiletto Snakes and Burrowing Asps)

Members of this genus have a unique feature – the venom. *Atractaspis'* venom comprises a series of amino-acid peptides called saraftoxins. This potentially lethal venom that has caused human fatalities.

For a long time Stiletto Snakes were thought to be members of the viper family due to their remarkably huge hollow fangs, which can be folded backwards. They have no other teeth except for two replacement fangs that sit next to the functional ones. Unlike vipers, however, Stiletto Snakes cannot project their fangs forward.

Special care must be taken if handling these snakes as they don't need to open their mouth to strike. They have a habit of swinging their mouth sideways and back – stabbing if held, as is the case when holding the majority of venomous snakes behind the head. Both fangs work independently from one another, so if it swings its jaw over to the left, the left fang will be exposed.

The Stiletto Snakes' fangs are placed to enable them to attack prey in a small burrow and earns them their other name of "mole vipers".

FAT STILETTO SNAKE
Atractaspis corpulenta
This stocky snake has smooth scales, with a narrow pointed head. The average length is 1 ft 4 in (40–50 cm), but their thick-set bodies earns their rather unflattering name! It lacks any sign of a neck with the head blending straight into the body. Its short tail has a little spine at the end. It has two color morphs – black or brown upperparts with either

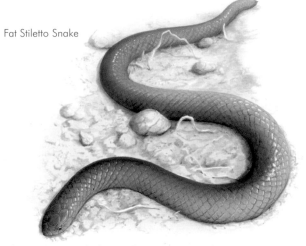

Fat Stiletto Snake

white or cream below. It lives in West Africa in semi-desert or grassland regions. It hunts primarily underground, using its ability to swing out a single fang to subdue animals in the confines of burrows. These include frogs, small mammals, other burrowing snakes and lizards. It lays clutches of usually 3–7 eggs. These snakes can give a very nasty bite but it is thought to be non-fatal to humans.

Genus *Chilorhinophis*
(Black and Yellow Burrowers)
All 3 species in this genus are black and yellow, hence their name. They come from Central, East and South Africa. These slender snakes have hardly any definition between head and neck, and the head appears very similar to its blunt-ended tail. They spend the majority of their time underground in tunnels under the forest floor.

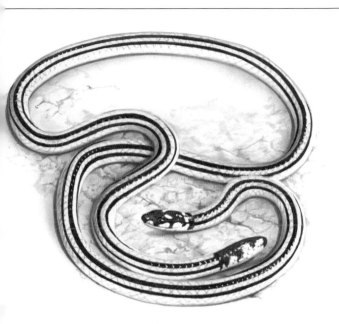

GERARD'S TWO-HEADED SNAKE

Chilorhinophis Gerardi

This fascinating snake has a very effective defense feature – confusion! Its tail mimics its head, making any predator think twice about which end to grab hold of. It has even been known to create false attacks by swiftly stabbing its tail in the direction of the intruder. This confusion gives the snake enough time to slip away. Its long, cylindrical, smooth-scaled body helps it to burrow through loose soil in search of food, mostly small worm lizards and snakes. This small oviparous snake, 1 ft 4 in (40 cm) long, is found in Zimbabwe north to the Democratic Republic of Congo.

Genus *Xenocalamus* (Quill-snouted Snakes)

There are 5 species in this beautifully bizarre genus. These small, gentle snakes grow to about 2 ft 8 in (80 cm) and live in Central and southern Africa. Their long, slender body, flattened head and acutely pointed snout make them exceptionally elegant snakes. They get their name from the shape of their head, which looks similar to an old-fashioned nib from a fountain pen or quill. They have a very large rostral (snout tip) scale and tiny eyes. Their diet consists mainly of amphisbaenians (worm lizards). All bear live young. Technically they are venomous. They don't bite, but a stab from their pointed nose might cause discomfort!

BICOLORED QUILL-SNOUTED SNAKE

Xenocalamus bicolor
This snake lives in deep sand, grows up to 2 ft (60 cm) and occurs in the northern regions of southern Africa. Its coloring is h i g h l y variable, with 4 b a s i c pattern and color phases. Females lay clutches of up to 4 eggs.

ELAPIDAE

This diverse family contains some of our most familiar, colorful, feared and deadliest of snakes. There are 60 genera containing 291 species All venomous Australasian snakes belong to this family. There are no vipers in Australasia (Australia and New Guinea), so the elapsids fill the ecological niche. They share many similarities with colubrids but differ in the dentition. Elapsids are all "proteroglyph" snakes, that is, they have fixed poison fangs at the front end of the upper jaw and they are therefore always erect and ready to be used for biting. Although more advanced than the back-fanged snakes, they are not as advanced as the folding fangs of the vipers. The venom gland drops its neurotoxic load down into the tooth through a hollow tube where it is delivered into the prey.

While at rest they keep their fangs in grooved slots in the lower jaw. Most elapsids prefer life on the ground; the exceptions are the tree cobras, water cobras, sea snakes and the arboreal mambas. The majority are egg-layers.

Fixed front fangs

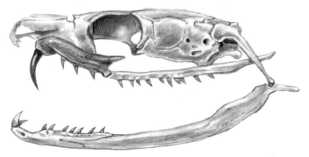

Genus *Acanthophis* (Death Adders)

How confusing! These snakes, of which there are 3 species, are not adders at all but members of the Elapidae family. All are found in Australia and New Guinea and as the latter is relatively unexplored, it is possible that more species will be discovered. These lumbering, chunky snakes are rather untypical for elapsids; in fact, they look and behave more like vipers. Instead of actively hunting their prey, they lie out of sight under leaf litter, waiting for their prey to come to them. It is for this reason that they are a real menace to humans; many people succumb to their camouflaged and deadly attacks. Death Adder numbers have suffered a dramatic drop in recent years; this is largely due to habitat change and the introduction of cats and foxes into their habitat. The introduced Cane Toad, *Bufo marinus,* probably causes the most damage. Young Death Adders play a large part in this enormous toad's appetite. Cane Toads also kill adults.

NORTHERN DEATH ADDER
Acanthophis praelongus

One of the main features of this stunning snake is its horns or rather, supraocular scales; these are the raised scales above their eyes. It lives in northern Australia and New Guinea and eats lizards and mammals, but tends to strike with an alarming speed at anything that comes its way. It grows up to 3 ft 3 in (1 m) but this is exceptional, 1 ft 8 in (50 cm) is more common. The Northern Death Adder as with all of the Death Adders uses a very smart technique to catch its prey. Its long, thin rat like tail, which is sometimes a different color to the rest of its body, is waved around in among the leaf litter. To an unsuspecting animal it may look like something to eat – a fatal mistake. The venom of this snake is exceptionally toxic. However, it does not attack unless provoked or stood on. Other species of death adders are the Common Death Adder, *A. antarcticus* and the Desert Death Adder, *A. pyrrhus.* The latter occurs in the remote deserts of central Australia. Its gorgeous reddish markings match the red soil and rocks of its habitat.

Genus *Austrelaps* (Australian Copperheads)

The only similarity with the American Copperheads, is the color of the head. They are not related at all. The American version belongs to the viper family, and as Australia has no vipers, their Copperheads belong to the elapsid family.

Although there are 3 species in this genus, Kangaroo Island Copperhead, *A. labialis,* Northern Copperhead, *A. ramsayi,* and the Southern Copperhead, *A. superbus*, some herpetologists believe that they are all variants of the one species. Copperheads are found in Victoria, Tasmania and the highlands of New South Wales and some Bass Strait islands. They survive on a diet of mainly frogs and lizards and all bear live young. All of the copperheads are highly venomous, but fatalities are rare as they are slow to strike and not very good at striking on target. They are the only venomous snake found above the snow line in Australia.

AUSTRALIAN COPPERHEAD

Austrelaps superbus

This beautiful snake is very much feared in Australia. This is because it lives in populated areas of Australia. It is a hardy snake and can bear cooler temperatures than many other snakes, which is why it emerges from hibernation early and is one of the last snakes to retreat in the winter. This thickset snake can have variable colorings from black to coppery brown. The scales get smaller towards its back and larger and lighter towards its underside. It can grow up to 4 ft 11 in (1.5 m), but this is rare. The main diet comprises mostly frogs and tadpoles, but they also eat lizards, snakes and rodents.

Genus *Boulengerina* (Water Cobras)

There are 2 species in this genus and they are the Banded Water Cobra, *B. annulata* and the Congo Water Cobra, *B. christyi*. These aquatic cobras all come from lakes of tropical Africa and can grow up to 8 ft 6 in (2.5 m). Although they possess the ability to flatten their hoods when threatened, like their large-hooded cousins, the result is not as marked. When not hunting in the water, these heavy, thick-set snakes spend their time half-hidden on riverbanks. They eat mainly fish. Though venomous it is not aggressive but it would rather move away than confront a human.

BANDED WATER COBRA

Boulengerina annulata

This beautiful snake is an excellent hunter in the water. A large, thick-set snake, it eats mainly fish.

Genus *Bungarus* (Kraits)

There are 12 species in this genus. If you live in southern Asia, southern China and Indonesia you might want to avoid these snakes. Kraits are highly venomous and are accountable for many snake-bite deaths. They may be encountered around human dwellings, probably because where you find humans you find rats and mice and other snakes, the kraits' favorite food. The Many-Banded Krait, *B. multicinctus* is the exception, as it eats mainly fish. At night they will venture inside buildings, taking on the job of pest control. For all their deadly venom, they are in fact rather shy and inoffensive, most bites occur when humans either roll over in their sleep and startle the snakes or stand on them in the dark. Kraits are hunted by the awesome King Cobra, which is impervious to the kraits' venom. When caught, some kraits try to coil and hide their heads, while others will thrash wildly. These smart snakes have a shiny, almost polished appearance. Some species may grow up to 6.5 ft (2 m), although they are normally shorter.

Kraits have an unusual body shape. They have a raised spine, which gives them a triangular shape.

Another peculiarity of kraits is their iris, which lacks any color: the eye has a very large pupil, an adaptation probably due to their nocturnal habits. All 12 species of kraits lay eggs.

The Common or Indian Krait, *B. caeruleus,* has incredibly strong venom; it is four times as potent as the Indian Cobra. Kraits are egg-layers.

BANDED KRAIT

Bungarus fasciatus

The longest of all the kraits, up to 6 ft 6 in (2 m), with a moderately slender shape and alternating bands of black and yellow (or cream). Its striking appearance is increased by the high dorsal ridge producing an unusual triangular body shape, giving rise to its local name "Triangular Snake". It is found in Indonesia, Southeast Asia and Malaysia. It is highly venomous to humans. As well as rodents it also preys on other snakes. Unlike the Malayan Krait, *B. candidus* the bands run around the snake's body.

Genus *Demansia* (Australian Whipsnakes)

These snakes are not related to the colubrid whipsnakes of Europe or North America. There are 8 species of *Demansia*, all of which are long, slender, elegant snakes. They live in Australia and southern New Guinea. They are agile, fast-moving snakes, active during the day. However, they may hunt on warm nights.

They occupy a wide range of habitat, ranging from rainforest to semi-desert. All are egg-layers and eat amphibians and reptiles. Venomous, but only the really large species are thought to be dangerous to humans.

YELLOW-FACED WHIPSNAKE

Demansia psammophis

This is a slender, fast-moving snake that is active during the day and is common throughout most of Australia. Its maximum length is 3 ft 3 in (1 m). Bites can cause serious localized swelling, but are rare, as these snakes prefer to avoid human encounters.

Genus *Elapsoidea* (African Garter Snakes)

Not to be confused with the North American garter snakes, *Thamnophis*. There are 8 species of African garter snakes, all of which are found throughout Africa south of the Sahara Desert. As all these snakes have similar markings, they can be tricky to identify. They burrow in sandy soil, coming to the surface at night where they hunt other reptiles, small mammals and frogs. They are venomous but not life-threatening to humans; bites can cause nausea, vomiting and dizziness.

SUNDEVALL'S GARTER SNAKE

Elapsoidea sundevallii

Slow-moving medium to large snake 3 ft 3 in (1m) long. Found in coastal forests, grassland and semi-desert across southern Africa. The juveniles are stunning, they have equally sized bold marks of cream or pink and rich chocolate-brown with a pale head and underside.

Genus *Dendroaspis* (Mambas)

There are 4 species in this genus: Eastern, *D. angusticeps,* Jameson's, *D. jamesoni,* West African Green, *D. viridis,* and the Black Mamba, *D. polylepis*. All lay eggs and hunt birds and small mammals. Although not true cobras, they do have a partial hood and will inflate it when threatened. The word "mamba" in Zulu means "big snake", which is exactly what they are. In fact the Black Mamba is Africa's largest venomous snake. The longest on record is 14 ft (4.2 m). Mambas certainly instill a great amount of fear in Africa. They are highly venomous but are not usually aggressive, they can, however, be rather unpredictable and very fast moving. There are many stories of mambas leaping from the undergrowth making unprovoked attacks on humans, but these are more likely to be derived from folklore. Mambas are egg-layers.

WEST AFRICAN GREEN MAMBA (see page 104)
Dendroaspis viridis
This is one of the 3 African Green Tree Mambas. It is a very bright green with a slightly yellowish tinge. It has a long elegant head with very large black eyes, which makes this snake quite distinctive. The smooth scales are unusually large, especially along its dorsal surface. It has large plate-like scales on the head offset by a darker skin color. It spends most of its time in trees, where it can be seen effortlessly moving from tree to tree, beautifully camouflaged and gracefully balanced. This quick-moving hunter eats mainly birds and occasionally bats. Although these snakes are reluctant to bite, they are highly venomous. Death follows quickly if not treated promptly.

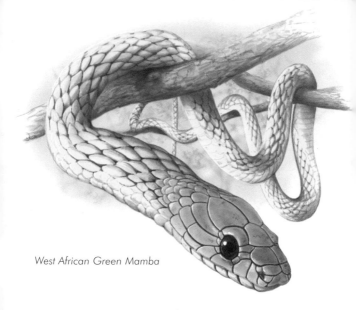

West African Green Mamba

BLACK MAMBA

Dendroaspis polylepis

This snake is thought to be far more dangerous and aggressive than the green mambas. It is the longest of all mambas, reaching an impressive 14 ft (4.3 m). It has an unusually toxic venom which is extremely fast-acting; death can occur within a few minutes of being bitten. The lethal neurotoxic venom is delivered by large fangs at the front of its long jaw. Some say it delivers enough venom in one bite to kill at least eight humans. What makes this an even more fascinating snake is the speed at which it can travel. It has been recorded at 9 mph (15 km/h). With its quick, deadly strike and amazing speed, the Black Mamba deserves respect. It prefers dry forest and brush or scrub hillsides. Though preferring life on the ground, it is a surprisingly good climber and can easily scale bushes and trees. It prefers either old rodent burrows or sometimes holes among rocks or old termite mounds for its shelter and these are rarely far from water. Squirrels, hyraxes, gerbils, other small mammals and birds are its favored foods. Because of its lightning-strike, it can even pluck passing birds from the air. At first glance, nothing about this snake seems black; the body color is normally a uniform gray-brown. When it opens its large mouth however, all is revealed — the inside is a striking purple-black color.

Genus *Hemachatus*

RINKHALS COBRA
Hemachatus haemachatus

There is only one species in this genus. Potentially it is a very dangerous snake with a lethal venom-spraying habit. It is restricted to South Africa and Zimbabwe and is the only spitting cobra found there. It is a stocky snake with a broad head and keeled scales. An unusual aspect of this snake is that instead of laying eggs, like other elapsids, it bears live

young. It grows to a maximum of 5 ft (1.5 m) and prefers open grassland and relatively dry areas. Juveniles are heavily banded, while some adults are a uniform dark brown.

The most feared feature is its venomous spray. Like other hooded cobras, when under threat it will rear its body from the ground, spread its hood and deliver a loud hiss. If this doesn't deter the antagonist, a fine spray of venom is released into the face, targeting the eyes. Venom can be sprayed up to a distance of about 10 ft (3 m). If on target, the venom will cause intense burning pain which leads to temporary or, in some cases, permanent blindness. As a further deterrent, if handled the snake can feign death by rolling onto its back with its mouth open.

In fact, spitting cobras don't really spit; they should really be called "spraying cobras" as that is what they do. When they open their mouth they forcibly exhale, releasing the venom from the venom glands through a tiny hole at the front of each fang.

Hunting takes place at night. However, they can be active on dull, overcast days. They eat other snakes, rodents, frogs and toads.

Genus *Micrurus, Micruroides* and *Leptomicrurus* (Coral Snakes from the New World)

These snakes are known for their bright colors and their extremely potent venom. Because of this, many non-venomous snakes mimic the bright colors of the coral snakes, falsely advertising to potential attackers that they too are highly venomous and should be avoided. New World coral snakes have a strong cannibalistic trait: not only do they eat other snakes, but they also seem to like eating their own species. All coral snakes lay eggs.

Starting with *Micrurus*, all 61 species from this genus come from North, Central and southern America. They range in size from 1 ft (45 cm) up to 4 ft 11 in (1.5 m). Normally found on the ground, their habitat varies from desert to lush forest. They eat mainly amphisbaenians (worm-lizards) as well as other reptiles.

There have been many human fatalities due to coral snakebites. Even though they have small mouths they are still capable of delivering their extremely dangerous venom. Handling with bare hands is a very stupid thing to do!

TEXAS CORAL SNAKE

Micrurus fulvius

Although quite common, the Texas Coral Snake is rarely seen. This slender snake has smooth, shiny scales and is typically brightly colored with a distinctive black snout. Behind this there is a large yellow band across its head. The rest of the body has large black and red bands, separated by thinner yellow ones. The red bands are usually spotted with black. It is found from Florida north to Carolina and west to Texas, it also occurs in parts of Mexico. Maximum

length is roughly 2 ft (75cm) but larger specimens have been recorded. It prefers dry, secluded habitats and usually hides by day under log piles, in old tree stumps or dense vegetation. It hunts at night and eats mainly frogs, lizards and other snakes. It lays 3–5 eggs per clutch. Beware, this snake can and will deliver an extremely dangerous bite. It is, however, a shy snake and if left alone will pose no threat. This species can be confused with the Scarlet Kingsnake, which is a harmless mimic.

SOUTHERN CORAL SNAKE
Micrurus frontalis

This Coral Snake is the most southerly species, occurring in South America from central Brazil to southern Argentina. Although there are many other similar-looking snakes in the region, this snake has a distinctive color banding: it has three black and two white bands between the red bands. What makes this snake unusual is its habit of laying its eggs in the nest of a specific ant, *Acromyrex lobicornis*. It even manages to lay its eggs in the fungus chamber which the ants keep at an almost constant humidity. The ants don't seem to mind this – they even clean the snake eggs, keeping them free from mold. Once the eggs hatch, the ants continue to protect the small snakes. One possible explanation for this seemingly symbiotic behavior could be that the young snakes eat would-be ant attackers, such as other snakes and worm lizards.

Genus *Micruroides*
One single species from America.

WESTERN CORAL SNAKE
Micruroides euryxanthus
This smooth-scaled, boldly colored coral snake has venom more powerful than that of any rattlesnake. However, because of their small mouth and fangs, some people believe they are incapable of biting humans effectively. Their range extends across Arizona, northern Mexico and southwest New Mexico. They like rocky upland deserts, especially where saguaro cactus is present. This small snake grows up to 25 in (63 cm) and is as thick as a pencil. Under threat it will make a popping sound by everting the lining of its cloaca.

Genus *Naja* (Cobra)

There are 17 species in this well-known genus. The King Cobra is not included in this group, it belongs in its own genus, *Ophiophagus*. The *Naja* cobras come from Africa and Southeast Asia. Cobras live in a range of habitats: deserts, forests, agricultural land, plantations and even towns and villages. When under threat, cobras will spread the skin around their necks into a hood. By doing so they can intimidate the enemy, by making themselves appear bigger. With the exception of the previously mentioned Rinkhals Spitting Cobra *Hemachatus haemachatus* (placed in its own genus), all cobras lay eggs. Some even stay with their clutches throughout incubation. All cobras have potentially lethal venom and if provoked can either inject or spit (depending on the species) their poison. Although they are responsible for many human deaths, they play such an important role in pest contral that the Indian government now protects cobras.

MONACLED COBRA

Naja kaouthis

Unlike the Spectacled Cobra, *Naja naja*, which has two round marks at the back of the hood, the Monacled has only one. A local legend attributes this mark to Buddha. It is said that when he awoke from a deep roadside meditation, he found a cobra shielding him from the harsh Indian sun. As a token of his appreciation he bent down and kissed the snake, leaving his mark for all the other cobras to see.

Snake charmers prefer to work with this snake as it is less aggressive than other cobras. Although it has fangs adapted to spitting, it rarely does. Many people believe that the cobra is being charmed by the music; in fact it is almost deaf to airborne sound. All the cobra is doing is following the swaying movement of the charmer, constantly aligning itself with its "target", in case it decides to strike. Some charmers cheat, they defang or sew up the mouths of their snakes, for although this is a relatively placid snake, its venom is lethal.

RED SPITTING COBRA

Naja pallida

The most startling aspect of this snake is its red color; it is the most colorful of all the cobras. This snake ranges from North Africa southeast to Tanzania and lives in dry, open grassland and scrub desert habitats. It can grow up to 5 ft (1.5 m). Its smooth, shiny scales come in a variety of reds. As the snake becomes older, the red gets deeper. The juveniles are really bright, and are incredibly conspicuous if seen out in the open. It eats other snakes, small mammals and birds.

Although this species has a hood, it is not very large and is only displayed if the snake is alarmed. When it lifts its head, neck and a small part of its body from the ground, a blackish-brown throat is revealed. The dark throat contrasts strongly with the snake's paler underside. Spittng cobras are well-adapted for targeting their prey. Their face tapers markedly towards the snout, with the broader part of the head behind the forward-facing eyes. Spitting is not always an option; when subduing prey, they will use their fangs.

INDIAN OR ASIATIC COBRA

Naja naja

This long, slender, smooth-scaled snake measures between 4–5 ft (1.3–1.6 m) long, although very rarely specimens of up to 7 ft (2.1 m) are found. Its hood can become very wide when alarmed. It has a wide range east and south through India, Sri Lanka and China. It is sometimes called "spectacled" cobra due to the bold white markings that look like "spectacles" on the back of the hood. This slender-looking snake is usually a very dark brown or black color with a paler underside, however, color variations are common. Although it can be found in almost any type of habitat, from forest to open grassland, it is often found in agricultural areas densely populated by people. It feeds chiefly on small mammals such as rats and mice. During the day the snake is more likely to retreat if disturbed. At night, however, it seems more aggressive; this could be due to better eyesight at night. Because this cobra likes to live close to humans, casualties are inevitable. Thousands of snake bites are reported each year, but it is thought that only one in ten cobra bites causes death.

Up to 24 eggs are laid in a rough scrape and both parents will stand guard, usually until the eggs hatch. Baby cobras are incredibly aggressive; if worried they can spread their hoods, just as their parents do, and deliver a dangerous bite. They are even capable of biting during and just after hatching.

Genus *Ophiophagu*

KING COBRA
Ophiophagus hannah

There is only one species in this genus and it is one of the most impressive snakes in the world. They are found from China to India, Southeast Asia, including Borneo and the Philippine archipelago. The King Cobra is the longest venomous snake on record. The longest was a staggering 18 ft 6 in (5.6 m), although they are usually smaller. It is so tall that when it rears up, sometimes up to half the length of its body, it can look an adult in the eye. Unlike other cobras it can move its whole body forward while standing up. It has been known to cover up to 10 ft (3 m) with each lunge. The amount of highly neurotoxic venom delivered in a single attack is also record-breaking. They have been known to kill working elephants in India. Not only does it bite, it has a tendency to chew, thus ensuring that a large dose of poison is well and truly injected. One record states it latched on for eight minutes to a tea worker, who died half an hour later. The worst time to find a King Cobra is while they are guarding their nests. They are fiercely protective of their eggs. If they are annoyed they will rear up, spread their small but long hood, and utter a deep hiss. Female King Cobras are the only snakes known to make a nest. She gathers leaves together using the coils of her body, and then makes two chambers, one for her and one for the eggs. The rotting plant vegetation keeps the eggs warm. King Cobra's main diet consists of other snakes. They even eat other poisonous snakes, such as kraits.

The King Cobra can rear up to a great height.

Genus *Notechis* (Australasian Tiger Snakes)

This genus has 2 species: the Black Tiger Snake, *N. ater* and the Common Tiger Snake, *N. scutatus*, sometimes called the Mainland Tiger Snake. They are found in southern Australia, Tasmania and smaller offshore islands. The two species can be divided into six main populations. Tiger snakes are highly venomous and are responsible for a high number of snake bites – many cause death. The main problem is that Tiger Snakes share the same territory as humans. Like other Australian elapsids they bear live young.

COMMON TIGER SNAKE
Notechis scutatus

This snake gets its name from its most common color and patterning, which is a gray-brown with yellow stripes. Sometimes these bandings and colors are not distinct and confusion can occur. A stout snake, it is usually about 3–4 ft (1.4 m) long but specimens up to 6 ft have been recorded. Although once a common snake, its numbers have been greatly reduced. If angry it can flatten out its neck but not form a hood. Frogs are its favorite food, although the adults may take small mammals as well; the juveniles eat frogs and tadpoles. A litter of about 40 is normal, although a female Black Tiger Snake is known to have given birth to 109 babies.

Genus *Oxyuranus*(Taipans)

Taipans are largest and most venomous of all Australian snakes. There are 2 species, the Taipan, *O. scutellatus,* from northern Australia and southern New Guinea, and the Inland Taipan or Fierce Snake, *O. microlepidotus.* The latter probably has a more placid nature, which is rather ironic considering its name. It is considered the world's most venomous snake.

One bite may carry enough venom to kill 12 men. It is just as well Inland Taipans are tucked away in the arid, central regions of Australia, well away from large populated areas.

INLAND TAIPAN OR FIERCE SNAKE

Oxyuranus microlepidotus

A long, slender, rather graceful snake capable of extremely quick movements. Usually up to 6 ft (2 m) long, although larger specimens have been recorded. Its head shape is similar to the Taipan but its neck is thicker and it has a greater slope from forehead to nose. Its black eyes are a little smaller than the Taipan's. Although there is a great deal of color variation, especially seasonal, the majority have dark brown to black heads. All forms have a yellow underside. Not much is known about the habits of this snake, partly due to its remote distribution. Whereas the Taipan will stab its prey with venom and wait until it dies, thus saving itself the possibility of damage, the Inland Taipan bites, then hangs on. Another difference is that the Taipan, if threatened, will defend itself by making repeated attacks, inflicting a mass of lethal bites. The Inland Taipan seems less inclined to attack.

BROWN AND BLACK SNAKES

There are 2 genera that make up this group of dangerously venomous snakes. As well as subduing their prey with venom, many are also constrictors, a feature more commonly associated with boas and pythons.

Genus *Pseudechis* (Black Snakes)

There are 6 species in this genus and all are egg-layers except the Red-bellied Black Snake. Sometimes referred to as brown snakes as well, due to the brown color variants. They will flatten their necks if cornered. These large snakes, sometimes up to 6 ft 6 in (2 m), eat frogs, lizards, snakes and small mammals. Not normally aggressive but potentially dangerous, owing to its highly toxic venom.

MULGA OR KING BROWN SNAKE

Pseudechis australis

This large, bulky snake can grow up to and over 8 ft (2.5 m). It has a very broad head and is generally quite slow-moving, but some snakes that occur in northern Australia can be far more excitable. Mulgas are found in most of Australia except the extreme south. Found over most woodland habitats but avoids swamps, it makes its home under logs, holes in or under rocks and in animal burrows. Depending on the climate it can be active both day and night. It's a common snake, if disturbed it can be reluctant to move away. Capable of producing a massive amount of venom, which has a devastating effect on other snakes and if not treated is lethal to humans.

RED-BELLIED BLACK SNAKE

Pseudechis porphyriacus

This snake has shiny black scales with an almost purple gloss when seen in sunlight. Underneath, the bright red is stronger on the outer ventral surface, becoming paler towards the center. Only found on the east coast and stretching down to the southeast corner of Australia, it prefers wet forests and swamps. This diurnal snake is naturally shy but if threatened it will flatten the neck and it may even attempt mock strikes. Diet consists of mainly frogs but also small mammals, lizards, and fish. It is known to be very cannibalistic. When handled it can produce a strong body odor.

Genus *Pseudonaja* (Brown Snakes)

There are 7 species in this genus. These are unpredictable, aggressive and potentially extremely dangerous snakes. They have small heads and relatively large eyes. A terrestrial genus that mainly preys on lizards, birds and small mammals. Once their prey is caught they will use venom and constriction to subdue it. Sometimes referred to as false cobras, because when annoyed, Brown Snakes will flatten their necks in a typical threat display. Oviparous, sometimes with clutches of over 30 eggs. All are from Australia and New Guinea.

EASTERN BROWN SNAKE

Pseudonaja textilis

This moderately large snake can grow up to about 7 ft (2 m). The venom is extremely dangerous and causes many fatalities in Australia. This is not a snake to mess with. It doesn't take much to annoy one. If given the chance, it will strike again and again as if in a blind frenzy.

SEA SNAKES

It seems hard to believe that during the process of evolution a branch of the elapsids took to the water and in some cases live a completely aquatic life. There are 17 genera of sea snakes with 63 species, split into two groups, the sea kraits, *Laticauda,* and the "true" sea snakes or Hydrophiinae, which means "water-lovers". Sea kraits have to come ashore to lay eggs, while the true sea snakes can give birth to live young in the sea and rarely need to leave its safety. Sea Kraits are banded, their common name comes from their resemblance to the banded land kraits of the genus *Bungarus.*

With the exception of three species, all live in the sea as opposed to fresh or brackish water. These snakes have several adaptations for a marine life: they have valves in their nostrils to exclude water, a salt excretion gland under the tongue, flattened bodies and paddlelike tails for propulsion through water. The amazingly long lung stretches to almost the whole length of the body, enabling them to stay underwater for up to half an hour. Most species maximum dive depth is 100 ft (30 m), although some may dive to roughly 500 ft (150 m). Sea snakes occur in all tropical seas of the Indian and Pacific oceans and many around the coast of northern Australia. They are absent from the Caribbean and the Atlantic Ocean. Stokes Sea Snake, *Astrotia stokesii* is the longest and heaviest, reaching 6 ft 6 in (2 m), although around 3–4 ft is more usual. Their rigid front fangs are capable of delivering some of the most toxic venom of all snakes. Luckily these snakes are not aggressive and are reluctant to bite. Divers frequently swim along side these snakes, without being bitten!

Genus *Laticauda* (Sea Kraits)

There are 5 species and all lay eggs which they come ashore to deposit. At night sometimes hundreds of snakes will invade islands and communally lay their eggs in caves, rocky outcrops or exposed coral. They can also be seen sunning themselves on warm rocks or floating driftwood. They have enlarged ventral scales like most land snakes.

YELLOW-LIPPED SEA KRAIT

Laticauda colubrina

This graceful snake grows up to 4 ft 11 in (1.5 m). It can be found around reefs and rocky shores off Southeast Asia, Australia, India and the Pacific islands. Fish, especially eels are its favored food.

Genus *Pelamis* (True Sea Snake)

The Yellow-bellied Sea Snake is the only species in this genus. It gives birth to live young at sea and is well adapted for aquatic life. It eats fish, especially eels, and can usually be found in shallow water.

YELLOW-BELLIED SEA SNAKE

Pelamis platurus

This unmistakable snake has unique markings and it is probably, out of all the sea snakes, the most highly adapted to a completely aquatic existence. It lacks the ventral scales used by land snakes to "crawl". Instead its tail is flattened and is used like a paddle, which makes it easier to speed through the water. It can be found feeding close to the surface of the water, especially in calm seas. The dark color on its back helps the snake absorb the heat from the sun. Its pale yellow belly may help it to hunt, as a fish looking up towards the sky is less likely to see the pale outline of the snake's body. This widespread snake is found throughout tropical waters from the east coast of Africa to the west coast of South and Central America.

Sometimes these snakes will amass in huge numbers – hundreds and some say thousands. They will drift with the current for miles. One theory is that this amassing allows the snakes to feed together more effectively; other theories suggest it is mating behavior.

VIPERIDAE

There are 4 subfamilies containing 30 genera and 228 species in this family. Vipers are considered to be the most advanced and highly evolved of all snake families. They are widespread around the world, except for Madagascar and Australasia, where they are absent. This is probably due to these areas splitting from the main landmass before vipers had a chance to evolve there. These intelligent snakes can be divided into 2 groups – those with and those without "pits". Pit vipers really are the peak of snake evolution; the facial pits (see page 14) means that they can hunt by sensing the heat of their prey. Vipers exhibit one major difference from cobras and their relatives and that is their fangs. They have incredibly large venom glands; this partly explains the characteristically wide head. These large venom glands are connected by ducts to two very large fangs, which have tubes in the center through which the venom is injected into the prey. Unlike cobras, there is no trace of the channel on the surface of the fang. The fangs of most vipers fold back and pivot independently of one another. These extra-long fangs help when subduing large prey as they enable the snake to deliver the venom deep into the victim. When the snake is ready to strike, it opens its mouth and muscle action rotates the maxillary bone on the which the fangs sit, so they flip forward and lock into place. Other unique features among vipers are the very sensitive heat sensors found on pit vipers' faces. Most species bear live young.

SUBFAMILY – AZEMIOPINAE

FEA'S VIPER
Azemiops feae

This genus contains only one species and that is the extremely rare Fea's Viper. It lives in the cloud forests of southern China, Vietnam and surrounding areas. Although little is known about this snake, it seems that its venom is fairly mild and that it eats small mammals. It is thought to be the most primitive viper. Its head is quite different from other vipers, it has large symmetrical plates, similar to elapsid and colubrid snakes

NIGHT ADDERS
SUBFAMILY – CAUSINAE

All 6 species are considered to be more primitive than other vipers due to their egg-laying and the arrangement of large scales on their heads. In fact they look more like colubrids than vipers. These nocturnal snakes rarely grow more than 3 ft 3 in (1 m) long, and have short, blunt heads and smooth scales. Most are brown with darker blotches, except for the Green Night Adder, C. *resimus*. All come from Africa and have a highly specialized diet of amphibians, especially frogs and toads. Mainly active at night, but you may find them basking in the daytime.

RHOMBIC NIGHT ADDER

Causus rhombeautus

This rather untypical viper is one of the few species that lay eggs, which is quite unusual among vipers. The most amazing feature about this snake is its huge venom glands. They are so large they extend down the neck, either side of the spine, for about 4 in (10 cm). Their venom is very effective on toads – their main food. In the unlikely event of a person being bitten, the pain and swelling is localized, and death is exceptionally rare. This ground-dwelling snake can be found across Africa, south of the Sahara. It has a tendency to make its home in vegetation, usually near water.

OLD WORLD VIPERS WITHOUT PITS
SUBFAMILY – VIPERINAE

Sometimes called the true vipers, there are 13 genera with 67 species, found throughout Africa, Asia and Europe. They are quite closely related to the Asian and American pit vipers, which includes rattlesnakes. The main difference from their New World counterparts is the lack of heat-sensitive pits on their face. Most live on the ground but will climb low bushes, with the exception of the African Bush Vipers *Atheris,* which are mostly arboreal.

Genus *Atheris* (Bush Vipers)

There are 10 species in this genus and most are arboreal, living in tropical African forests. Their short, round head, large eyes and strongly keeled scales make them very distinctive. They have dangerous bites but only the Green Bush Viper, *A. squamiger*, is known to have caused death. Bush vipers are viviparous, giving birth to up to 10 young.

HAIRY BUSH VIPER

Atheris hispida

Its other name is Rough-scaled Viper. This bizarre-looking snake has heavily keeled and extremely elongated scales which stick up at the tips. This effect makes this snake look like it has been pulled through a bush backwards. Juveniles have yellow eyes, whereas the adults have large, cute-looking black eyes. This distinctive snake is usually a pale blue-green, but it can have a yellow wash towards the tips and in the centre of its scales. It bears live young and eats frogs and lizards.

Genus *Bitis* (African Adders)

There are 14 species in this highly venomous genus. All have stout bodies and broad triangular heads. They vary in size from around 3–6 ft 6 in (1–2 m). All are strictly terrestrial, epitomizing the sit and wait hunter, and for this reason they are responsible for many human deaths in Africa. They give birth to live young, sometimes up to 100.

PUFF ADDER

Bitis arietans

So called because of its habit of puffing up when angry. It grows up to 3 ft 4 in (1 m), is stout and has a very short tail. The yellowy-brown color (highly variable) is decorated with bold black chevrons, each with a white trailing edge,

running down the back. Their coloring is ideal camouflage when lying among leaf litter or grass and they are masters of ambush hunting. They give birth to up to 50 young and eat mainly rodents. Occurs in many habitats except rainforest, preferring drier habitats. Some species that occur in semi-desert scrub are naturally paler.

GABON VIPER OR ADDER

Bitis gabonica

Like the Puff Adder, the Gabon Viper is very well adapted for lying buried in the leaf litter. The eyes are positioned on top of the head and the nostrils are on top of the snout. Its markings even look like dead leaves. It lives in the rainforests of West and Central Africa. This massive viper grows to about 6 ft 7 in (2 m) but its girth is incredibly thick sometimes around 15 in (40 cm). When annoyed it can make itself much thicker by puffing itself up, like the Puff Adder. Because of its markings it is almost impossible to see it until too late. When these snakes do strike, it is with lightning speed and because they have the longest fangs of any snake in the world (sometimes up to 2 in (5 cm), their highly toxic

The bold black and white markings on this Puff Adder are obvious.

This Gabon Viper's markings make it very difficult to see when in leaf litter.

venom enters deeply into the prey.

Their heads are very large, containing the huge venom glands and enormous fangs. This awesome snake can take prey as large as small antelopes. It has even been said that it can eat porcupines, although it normally eats smaller forest mammals. Some specimens almost lack the two horns on the tip of the nose, while others have very long and pronounced "horns". It seems that the farther west you travel in Africa, the bigger the horns become. Gabon vipers give birth to up to around 60 live young.

RHINOCEROS VIPER

Bitis nasicornis

Because of its preference for damp habitats this snake's other name is the "Riverjack". Although similar in habits to the Gaboon Viper, it is much brighter colored. The intricate patterns include a row of light blue bow tie-shaped markings running along the length of its rich purple-brown body. The flanks are paler, sometimes with yellow markings. It has two very large "horns" on the end of its snout. They are in fact a cluster of enlarged scales. Rarely exceeds 3 ft 6 in (1 m). Found in the forests of West Africa, particularly along riverbanks. Up to 60 live young. Eats small mammals and birds.

Genus *Cerastes* (North African Desert Vipers)

All these snakes have heavily keeled scales and are capable of giving a very nasty, although rarely fatal, bite. There are 3 species in this genus. They are the Arabian Horned Viper, *C. gasperettii*, Sahara Horned Viper, *C. vipera* and Desert Horned Viper. Like many desert snakes, they all move by sidewinding. These relatively short snakes lay eggs and live in North Africa and the Middle East.

DESERT HORNED VIPER

Cerastes cerastes

The most distinctive feature of this snake is its two horns. Although no one is quite sure why they are there, it is assumed that their purpose is to protect their eyes. When the snake hunts it lies half to almost completely submerged in the sand, with sometimes only the two horns barely

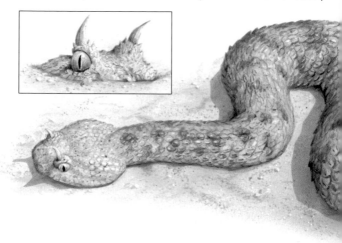

visible. The horns stop the sand from building up over the eyes, they also act as a visor, shading the snake from the harsh desert sun. In fact several desert vipers all over the world have large, eyebrowlike scales above their eyes.

The Desert Horned Viper, however, has the largest horns of any. This amazing snake is the master of disguise, and its coloring is the exact match of its sandy or stony-desert home. Its colors vary from dirty yellow-brown to a pale buff and cream with darker scattered blotches running along its back. These markings do a fantastic job of breaking up the outline of the snake, making it impossible to detect for an unsuspecting passing lizard or rodent.

Sometimes called the "Horned Asp", these vipers rarely exceed 2 ft (60 cm) and lay an average of 20 eggs. Their heavily-keeled scales help the snake move across sand. When annoyed they can rub their rough scales together to make a loud rasping noise.

Genus *Daboia* (Russell's Viper)

RUSSELL'S VIPER

Daboia russellii

Although not a pit viper, it has highly developed facial nerve endings. This beautiful viper has a wide head covered with small overlapping keeled scales and a rounded snout with big nostrils. The brown oval markings are fringed with black and extend in a straight line along its back. This species is common from Pakistan to China and Indonesia. Active mainly during the day, this snake becomes very aggressive when annoyed; it has a deadly lightning strike and is the cause of a huge number of human snake bites which, if untreated, may prove fatal. Before it strikes it will emit a very loud hissing noise as a deterrent; if this doesn't work a strike with great force follows.

142

Genus *Echis* Carpet or Saw-scaled Vipers

All of the 8 species in this genus are live-bearing and extremely dangerous. Although all are fairly small, usually under 3 ft (1 m) their abundance, camouflage and potent venom make these some of the most feared snakes in the world. Saw-scaled Vipers are so-called because of their serrated scales on the lower flanks which they rub together while performing a figure-of-eight, coiled threat display. Coupled with the rasping sound made by the scales and the snake's loud hissing, this viper has a very impressive threat display.

EASTERN CARPET VIPER OR SAW-SCALED VIPER

Echis carinatus

This small, slender viper has a pear-shaped head, a short, rounded snout and eyes situated towards its snout. It bears around 20 live young, and is about 1 ft 11 in (60 cm)

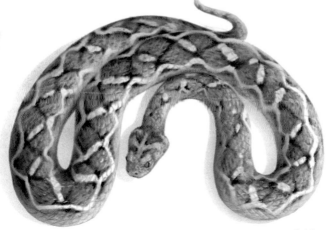

long. It eats mainly lizards and small mammals but will take amphibians and invertebrates. The Latin word *Echis* means "X", which refers to the distinctive marking on the top of these snakes' head. Beware, this marking varies and is not always present. Its preferred habitat is dry open grassland, semi-desert, rocky areas and lightly wooded places. More than any other desert viper, this snake is able to endure the heat of direct sun. Its impressive defense display includes inflating its body so the serrated scales stick out of the sides of its body, then throwing itself into a horseshoe shape, rubbing its looped body against itself. Its very nervous disposition means that if it is worried a strike is almost inevitable. In fact, it will sometimes carry out frenzied repeated attacks. Its incredibly potent hemotoxic venom causes massive bleeding and severe pain. Due to its wide range, from India through the Middle East to East Africa, snake bites and fatalities are common.

Genus *Vipera*

Currently there are 25 species in this wide-ranging, varied genus. Their range varies from northern Scandinavia, where the Adder, *Vipera berus* occurs, to Japan and south to Taiwan, where a form of Russell's Viper, *V. russelli formosensus* lives. They live in a wide range of habitats: from mountains or semi-desert, to moors, scree slopes, forests and open heathland. They all bear live young. Predominantly terrestrial but some occasionally climb, although never very high. They feed on lizards, small mammals and invertebrates.

NOSE-HORNED VIPER OR SAND VIPER
Vipera ammodytes
This wide-headed viper has keeled scales with a prominent fleshy horn on the tip of its snout. The Nose-horned Viper is sexually dimorphic, which means the sexes look different. Males tend to be brighter and more boldly marked, sometimes a striking silver and black, while females are normally a brownish-red with darker markings. The characteristic dark, zigzag markings run down the back from the neck to the tip of the tail. Some snakes have a different color to the tip of their thin tapering tail which may be used for luring prey. Found in dry, sandy or rocky places, it eats lizards, birds and small mammals and gives birth to between 5–15 live young.

ADDER
Vipera berus

Known also as the Northern Viper, this snake ventures farther north than any other snake and occurs well into the Arctic Circle. It also has the widest geographic range, occurring from western Europe across northern Asia to the Pacific coast. The Adder has a variety of body colors across its range, varying from gray, brownish or reddish; but all have the characteristic zigzag stripe running along the vertebral line from the neck to the tip of the tail. Sometimes Adders are completely black; this color variation is more common in the north of the range where the dark coloring helps the snake absorb the warmth from sunlight. Although a hardy snake, sometimes emerging from hibernation as early as February, it is not until April that mating occurs. Males will defend their territories and their right to mate. Males will rear up attempting to push the other male to the ground. The stronger snake wins while the other retreats.

Adders are Britain's only venomous snake. However, effects from Adder bites vary from hardly noticeable to a week in the hospital. Very occasionally deaths occur if the victim is allergic to the venom. These gentle snakes will only bite if stood on; in fact in the UK it is more likely that you will be struck by lightning than bitten by an Adder.

SUBFAMILY – CROTALINAE (PIT VIPERS)

Pit vipers have a superficial resemblance to the Viperinae, or Old World vipers. Obviously the big difference is the large (larger than the nostril), prominent, heat-sensitive pit situated on each side of the head. If you draw a line between the nostril and the eye the facial pits lie just below it. These heat-sensing pits provide the snake with a highly accurate targeting system for hunting warm-blooded animals in the dark. Pit Vipers are found in both the New World (North, Central and South America) and Old World (Africa and Asia). There are 18 genera containing about 154 species. There is a great deal of variety throughout this subfamily: some snakes are arboreal, while others live entirely on the ground. The majority are viviparous but some lay eggs. Some are very brightly colored, while others are dull. All of these snakes are potentially dangerous to humans.

Genus *Agkistrodon*

There are 10 species in this genus, three of which occur in North America and two of those are well-known and potentially dangerous to humans. The 3 American species occur in southeastern USA and Central America. They are the Copperhead, *A. contortrix*, the Cottonmouth, *A. piscivorus* and the Cantil, *A. bilineatus*. The rest occur throughout Asia. These medium-sized snakes rarely exceed 3 ft 6 in (1 m). They all give birth to live young. They feed on a variety of prey ranging from fish, frogs, small mammals and birds to carrion.

COTTONMOUTH

Agkistrodon piscivorus

The Cottonmouth is unique among vipers in being semi-aquatic and it is for this reason it is also known as the Water Moccasin. It is a heavy-bodied snake whose body color varies from black, dark brown to gray. It has weakly keeled scales with either dark or cream barring along its body. Some snakes have a thin cream line running from the snout to above the eye. The head is obviously thicker than its body. Confusion with water snakes is common; it is important to look for the facial pits which lie between the eye and the nose, the vertical pupils and the position of the eye. Water snakes have eyes that are visible from the top of their heads while the Cottonmouth's eyes are more towards the sides of the head. The Cottonmouth swims with its head out of the water, while water snakes submerge their heads. It is worthwhile trying to identify the differences between the Cottonmouth and harmless water snakes. The Cottonmouth is potentially an extremely dangerous snake, and should be given a wide berth if found. It is very nervous and is capable of giving a fatal bite. If annoyed it will stand its ground, repeatedly gaping its mouth, showing the bright white lining, which is why it is called the Cottonmouth. If you are sensible you will retreat before it delivers a highly venomous bite. If picked up, it has an additional defense mechanism – it can produce a foul-smelling, musky aroma which has been likened to a billy goat.

The Cottonmouth can be found around a variety of water habitats from lowland swamps to mountain streams. It eats fish, frogs, salamanders, turtles and even birds. They have been observed feeding on migrant warblers, including Yellow and Wilson's Warblers. It will also scavenge from carrion.

COPPERHEAD

Agkistrodon contortrix

The distinctive markings of this stout, North American pit viper make it a very handsome snake. Their body color varies from copper or pinkish-brown but all have bold chestnut crossbands which can resemble an hourglass shape, running along the length of the body. These markings start at the tail and stop just short of the head, which is unmarked and not always a copper color. Copperheads, usually juveniles, have a yellowy-green tip to their tail which helps them to hunt. The tail end is twitched whilst the snake lies hidden in leaf litter. Any small passing animal will find this curious and will investigate, usually with fatal consequences. Adults have a characteristically triangular head and upturned nose. Copperheads are related to rattlesnakes and share a similar habitat. Typical summer retreats for the Copperhead are stone walls, piles of wood, rotting logs, mounds of disused farm debris and large flat stones near streams where they can sometimes be seen sunning themselves. Their homes are never too far away from water: either rocky outcrops above streams or edges of swamps and ponds. This can lead to confusion with water snakes, just look for the large head and facial pits of the Copperhead. Mating occurs in April after they emerge from hibernation. Between four and eight young are born from July to August. When the weather turns cooler in the fall, they return to their winter den to hibernate. Sometimes they will share their dens with many other snakes including the Timber Rattlesnake.

The Copperhead is not an aggressive snake and will try very hard to avoid confrontation. Its camouflage makes this easier to achieve, although if trodden upon it will inflict a venomous bite.

Genus *Bothrops* (Fer-De-Lances or Lanceheads)
There are 41 species in Latin America, so called because of
the lance or spear-head shape of their head. All are
extremely venomous. Envenomation produces massive
bleeding and without treatment, death is almost certain.
They are large snakes, growing up to 8 ft (2.4 m).

FER-DE-LANCE
Bothrops atrox
This chunky snake has a sharp, pointed snout and grows to
a maximum of 5 ft (1.5 m). Its keeled scales are brown or
gray with darker blotches and lighter streaks. A pair of dark
brown stripes running from behind the eye to the back of the
head is characteristic. Typically terrestrial, but some
(particularly juveniles) are occasionally found in trees.

Genus *Bothriopsis*

Known collectively as the palm vipers, all species are largely arboreal. They have a heat-sensitive organ between the eye and the nostril, which is used to find prey in the dark of the rainforest.

EYE-LASH VIPER

Bothriopsis schelegii

This *incredibly* variable colored snake has a broad, flat, triangular head with small eyes and vertical pupils, and a patch of bristly scales over each eye – hence the name. It may be green or yellow in color and can have a mottled pattern that resembles lichen. It is found from southern Mexico to northern South America in tropical rainforests. This species has a prehensile tail, which allows it to hang motionless in the trees waiting for its favorite prey of birds, small mammals and frogs.

Genus *Crotalus* (Rattlesnakes)

There are about 32 species of rattlesnakes, so called because of their ability to rattle the end of their tails. The terminal, interlocking tail segments are dead and hollow and when shaken produce the characteristic sound.

EASTERN DIAMONDBACK RATTLESNAKE

Crotalus adamanteus

This is the largest and most dangerous of all the rattlesnakes, it can be up to 6 ft 7 in (2 m) long, it is probably the most venomous snake in the USA. It occurs in southeastern USA from north Carolina west to Louisiana. Be careful, this snake has a tendency to stand its ground and can be aggressive if provoked.

SIDEWINDER

Crotalus cerastes

The Sidewinder is a rattlesnake that is very well adapted to a desert lifestyle. It can move rapidly across the desert, leaving only strange single lines on the surface. This species parallels many of the side-winding vipers found in North Africa and the Middle East. They have horns over their eyes and have a similar mode of travel over the shifting desert sands. The snake anchors its head and tail in the sand and lifts its trunk free of the ground, moving sideways. This action is then repeated, causing a fast forward movement. The sideways motion of the sidewinder results in only a small section of the body touching the sand at any one time, a useful strategy if the sand is hot.

Genus *Lachesis*
BUSHMASTER

Lachesis muta

The Bushmaster is the only species in this genus. They are the largest of all the vipers. These huge snakes have been recorded at just over 12 ft (3.6 m) long, which makes them the largest venomous snake in the New World. The more usual adult size is 8 ft (2.4 m). These snakes come from southern Central America and northern South America. This is a formidable snake; not only does its length, weight and large head make it impressive, it also carries a massive amount of very potent venom which it delivers with great force. Its scientific names mean "silent fate", referring to its sit-and-wait hunting method, and although a great name for a potentially lethal hunter, it is not completely accurate. When alarmed the Bushmaster will shake the hard tip of its tail which produces a buzzing sound.

**Genus
Tropidolaemus**

WAGLER'S PIT VIPER

Tropidolaemus wagleri

This big-headed, bulky and beautiful snake is very variable in color. It may be green, turquoise, or black with bars of yellow and light green. The young lack any black markings, and are a bright green with red and white spots. They all have a brown stripe that runs through the eye. This Old World pit viper is common in parts of Southeast Asia, such as Indonesia, Philippines, Thailand and Malaysia. They are famous for living in the Buddhist snake temple on the island of Penang, where they are kept on display. These pit vipers are highly venomous. They eat frogs, mammals and lizards. Adults are around 3 ft 4 in (1 m). They give birth to about 15–40 live young.

INDEX

BY LATIN NAME